For my friends
Kevin Roy and Norman Grimbeek

JUSTIFICATION: A GUIDE FOR THE PERPLEXED

T&T Clark *Guides for the Perplexed*

T&T Clark's Guides for the Perplexed are clear, concise and accessible introductions to thinkers, writers and subjects that students and readers can find especially challenging. Concentrating specifically on what it is that makes the subject difficult to grasp, these books explain and explore key themes and ideas, guiding the reader towards a thorough understanding of demanding material.

***Guides for the Perplexed* available from T&T Clark**

Balthasar: A Guide for the Perplexed, Rodney Howsare
Benedict XVI: A Guide for the Perplexed, Tracey Rowland
Calvin: A Guide for the Perplexed, Paul Helm
Christian Bioethics: A Guide for the Perplexed, Agneta Sutton
Christology: A Guide for the Perplexed, Alan Spence
De Lubac: A Guide for the Perplexed, David Grumett
Eucharist: A Guide for the Perplexed, Ralph N. McMichael
Martyrdom: A Guide for the Perplexed, Paul Middleton
Pannenberg: A Guide for the Perplexed, Timothy Bradshaw
Process Theology: A Guide for the Perplexed, Bruce Epperly
Sin: A Guide for the Perplexed, Derek R. Nelson
Theological Anthropology: A Guide for the Perplexed, Marc Cortez
Tillich: A Guide for the Perplexed, Andrew O'Neill
The Trinity: A Guide for the Perplexed, Paul M. Collins
Wesley: A Guide for the Perplexed, Jason E. Vickers

Forthcoming titles

Political Theology: A Guide for the Perplexed, Elizabeth Philips

JUSTIFICATION: A GUIDE FOR THE PERPLEXED

ALAN J. SPENCE

t&t clark

Published by T&T Clark International
A Continuum Imprint
The Tower Building, 11 York Road, London SE1 7NX
80 Maiden Lane, Suite 704, New York, NY 10038

www.continuumbooks.com

British Library Cataloguing-in-Publication Data
A catalogue record for this book is available from the British Library

ISBN: 978-0-567-41085-6 (Hardback)
       978-0-567-07751-6 (Paperback)

Typeset by Newgen Imaging Systems Pvt Ltd, Chennai, India
Printed and bound in India

CONTENTS

List of Abbreviations   viii

Introduction   1

Chapter 1   The Human Predicament in Western
            Christian Thought   5

Chapter 2   Divine Judgement in the New Testament   17

Chapter 3   Augustine of Hippo   30

Chapter 4   Thomas Aquinas   44

Chapter 5   Martin Luther   59

Chapter 6   John Calvin   76

Chapter 7   Friedrich Schleiermacher   92

Chapter 8   Karl Barth   109

Chapter 9   A New Perspective   127

Chapter 10 Justification Today   146

Notes   160

Selected Bibliography   164

Index   167

LIST OF ABBREVIATIONS

ANF   *Ante-Nicene Fathers*, reprinted by William B. Eerdmans (Grand Rapids, MI, 1985)

NPNF *Nicene and Post-Nicene Fathers*, reprinted by William B. Eerdmans (Grand Rapids, MI, 1975)

INTRODUCTION

There is one striking sentence in a letter that Paul wrote to the newly formed church in Rome that captures something of both the paradox and the potency of the idea of justification.

> However, to the man who does not work but trusts God who justifies the wicked, his faith is credited as righteousness. (Rom. 4.5 NIV)

It certainly sounds odd to suggest that God justifies those who live wickedly. Some might wonder how one could be expected to trust in a judicial system where judges regularly acquit the guilty. Such a way of behaving, when applied to God, appears to undermine all that theists hold to be true about divine justice and the ethical nature of the universe. Surely God must, because of the righteousness of his being, uphold the cause of the innocent rather than the guilty, the righteous rather than the unrighteous? How on earth can we trust a god who justifies the wicked? Yet within this perplexing notion we also catch a glimpse of the power that a doctrine of justification has to provide a lifeline of hope to those who find themselves adrift in the sea of moral failure and personal guilt. For those who regret that their lives have been compromised by sin and who are ashamed of their participation in its dark designs, the promise of justification comes as unimaginable good news.

No other concept in the history of the Church has given rise to so large a body of learned literature; has evoked so much passion and controversy and has tragically fuelled an inter-Christian conflict of so implacable a nature. In the sixteenth and seventeenth centuries many Christians came to believe that their particular doctrine of justification encapsulated the essence of God's saving action, that it lit up, as it were, the God-given path from death to life. Others felt that such an interpretation of the scriptures was no more than a license to lawlessness, undermining all true godliness and moral accountability. It is no wonder that the discussion generated such intense heat in its time.

The fires of this religious controversy have, of course, long since died down. As they kick around among its remaining embers many students today will struggle to conceive how sensible persons of faith could once have been prepared to risk their lives in the ravages of war or go to the stake in defence of this particular view of salvation. For the past century or so most theologians have held that there are a number of ways that the atonement is portrayed in the scriptures and that justification is but one of the metaphors or models that the New Testament employs to disclose the mystery of the cross. It is, therefore, quite hard for the majority of modern enquirers to examine the carefully nuanced exposition of this doctrine in earlier debates without an element of impatience or even condescension. The enormous energy spent on them seems to have been sadly misplaced. It is generally only historical theologians or those with a strong commitment to particular confessional traditions who appear to be at all interested in trying to understand the ideas motivating this ancient discussion.

Why is this? How can a subject that once held so central place in the confessions of all the early Protestant churches and in the formulations of the Roman Catholic Reformation, now find itself on the periphery of theological interest? One answer is that the context has changed. A doctrine of justification is generally no longer recognized as resolving the most pressing religious needs of the community. Let us consider this idea a little more closely. It would seem that there is a close relation between our understanding of the human predicament and our interpretation of divine deliverance, for salvation by its nature is rescue from some sort of problem confronting us. A theory of salvation that does not resolve a perceived threat to human well-being makes as much sense as a drug that has been developed to cure a disease from which no one suffers.

Historical theology gives strong support to the idea that every interpretation of salvation is directly related to a particular understanding of the human condition. The Eastern Church has tended to view the human plight in terms of spiritual blindness, bondage to the forces of evil, along with moral and physical corruption. Corresponding to this, it has interpreted salvation using concepts such as spiritual enlightenment, redemption from demonic power and participation in the divine life. On the other hand, the particular concern of the Western Church has been on the ubiquitous and recalcitrant nature of human sin and the alienation from a holy God and prospect of divine judgement that it entails. Alongside this, salvation has been understood in the West primarily in terms of forgiveness, mercy and divine reconciliation. And it is only in a world-view shaped by these concepts that a doctrine of justification makes sense. When concerns about sin, alienation and final judgement are no longer an integral aspect of the prevailing religious mind-set, the doctrine, as it has been expounded historically, is bound to lose its persuasive force or spiritual relevance.

This means that if we are to embark on a study of the doctrine of justification with an eye to the way it functions as a theory of salvation, we require at least some understanding of the predicament which it claims to resolve, in this case, the problem of guilt and the prospect of divine judgement on human sinfulness. Examining the meaning of justification in abstraction from the corresponding human condition would be like trying to comprehend the technical workings of a kidney dialysis machine without any reference to renal failure.

There are then two aspects to our study of justification. We need to examine the underlying human plight and we need to understand how such a condition is resolved by divine justification.

Historically, the doctrine of justification has flourished in the West where the human predicament has been shaped by concerns with of sin and accountability before God. Our study begins with a consideration of the way these ideas have fashioned Western thought. We will take a guided tour of the imagination through a gallery of the some of the most significant works of art in Western culture, works of literature, poetry, painting and sculpture and allow them to disclose to us the way in which these concepts became integral to a Western world-view. The scriptural foundation of this world-view will be evaluated in the light of the testimony of the New Testament, in particular, the recorded parables and sayings of Jesus and the structure of Paul's argument in his letter to the Romans.

As your 'tour guide' it might be helpful at this stage to offer a word of encouragement to the reader who might be feeling a little apprehensive. The concept of divine judgement has been so parodied in modernity that there is a temptation to avoid the subject in much the same way that one might give a wide berth to the man on the high street clad in sandwich boards announcing that 'The end is nigh'. The matter is, however, worthy of closer attention than that. Oliver O'Donovan has argued persuasively that the act of judgement has to do with the revelation of truth: a determination of what actually happened and the appropriate consequences of such action. 'Since an act of judgment is true by correspondence to the act on which it reflects, punishment is an "expressive" act, telling the truth about an offense' (*The Ways of Judgement*, p. 110). The perception that divine judgement is an unveiling of truth might encourage the cautious student to lay aside the prevailing caricatures and approach the subject with renewed interest and openness.

The second and more significant purpose of our study is to try and determine what Paul meant by justification and to consider how it resolves the human predicament. We will 'listen in' on key moments of the rich and complex discussion that has been taking place between the principal interpreters of Paul's doctrine of justification in the Western tradition these past 1,500 years. My hope is that through a careful attentiveness to some of the salient features of that debate and by a critical engagement with them, we will be better equipped to return finally to the texts themselves and provide an informed outline of Paul's own meaning.

We begin then with an exploration of the part played by the ideas of sin, alienation and final judgement in shaping Western thought.

CHAPTER 1

THE HUMAN PREDICAMENT IN WESTERN CHRISTIAN THOUGHT

From an early stage, perspectives which emphasized the ideas of sin, estrangement from God and divine judgement came to determine the spirituality of the Western Christian community. How did this happen? Where did these ideas come from? What was the outworking of such concepts in religious thought and practice? In seeking to better understand these matters we will briefly consider some significant works of Christian literature and art, works that not only offer us a window into Western concerns with the ideas of sin and judgement but, more significantly, have played a major role in shaping them.

AUGUSTINE'S CONFESSIONS

Augustine of Hippo (354–430) stands astride Western theological thought as an intellectual Colossus, giving shape and direction to nearly all of its major themes. He is of particular significance for this study in that he championed a doctrine of original sin. He argued that our universal tendency to wrongdoing as well as our moral blameworthiness is inherited from our first parents. One of the consequences of this solidarity in sin, according to Augustine, was that although we have freedom of the will, it is a freedom which has now been made captive. We cannot of ourselves choose what is truly good apart from divine grace. Our free-will which has been imprisoned through sin must now be liberated if we are to turn willingly to God.

These powerful and provocative ideas, developed in Augustine's extensive polemic with the Manicheans on the one hand and the

Pelagians on the other, have continued to influence Christian discussions on the nature of sin, free-will and the way of salvation. But the text which perhaps offers the most rewarding insight into Augustine's view of a Christian's personal response to the problem of sin is his *Confessions*. It was written in the form of a prayer to God around AD 397 when Augustine was some 43 years old. Its literary style, however, is not simply, as one might have expected, that of a penitent seeking absolution. It is rather a spiritual autobiography. It is Augustine's story of his life from his birth to his conversion to the Christian faith, soon followed by the death of his mother. Some consider it to be the first significant autobiographical work in Western literature, giving shape to the whole literary genre.

But the form of the *Confessions* is also somewhat different from autobiographies as we now know them. Rather, it can be likened to the ruminations of a man who is alone with his lover sharing the history of his infidelities. It is for him, paradoxically, a rewarding rather than distressing and humiliating exercise because he is certain both of her total forgiveness and of her absolute love. To be honest and open at last about his somewhat sordid history is a great relief. There is no reason to hide anything that is false, mean or dirty in all of his affairs, because each of them now serve only to highlight the beauty, purity and perfection of the present relationship. Changing metaphors, one could say that the *Confessions* function as a sort of moral audit in the presence of God, not so much about the sins of the body, but of the ideas and philosophies that Augustine flirted with and was captivated by. It is a wholehearted 'coming clean' in the light of all that he, as a Christian, now holds to be true.

> What return shall I make to the Lord for my ability to recall these things with no fear in my soul? I will love you, Lord, and thank you, and praise your name, because you have forgiven me such great sins and such wicked deeds.[1]

In this cleansing process Augustine alludes to his theory of the nature of evil. He holds that evil is in essence the absence of the good. It does not have any final reality or substance of its own. This means that Augustine's sins are always viewed as the distortion of what is true, as the perversion of something positive. 'I did not know that evil is nothing but the removal of the good until finally no good remains.'[2] 'And when I asked myself what wickedness was, I saw that it was not a substance but a perversion of the will when it turns aside from you.'[3] Consequently, Augustine's sins, properly considered, inevitably point him back to the good, that is, back to God. This directing back to the good, along with his obvious love for God, is what enables the *Confessions* to be such a positive and affirming spiritual treatise. Personal sin is, of course, highly problematic, but it is a problem that has been resolved by grace and is for Augustine, through confession and repentance, an occasion for experiencing the richness of divine love.

> I must now carry my thoughts back to the abominable things I did in those days, the sins of the flesh which defiled my soul. I do this, my God, not because I love those sins, but so that I may love you. For love of your love I shall retrace my wicked ways.[4]

It would appear that this focus on sin and confession which Augustine's theology helped to encourage in the Western Church was, at least in his case, a far more positive and constructive spiritual exercise than we are now generally inclined to think. Confession of sin was for him liberating and empowering rather than demeaning; it encouraged confidence rather than guilt, praise and love for God rather than self-absorption or self-loathing. What begins as confession of sin, soon becomes for him the confession of God's graciousness. Such an awareness of personal sin, along with the appropriate penitential response to it, came to be emphasized in the Church as a key aspect of the process of salvation.

Further, the *Confessions* offered a paradigm of the Christian as one who had undertaken a spiritual journey from darkness to light. In doing so it focused attention on the question of how salvation is to be attained. It is interesting that not long after the publication of the *Confessions* Augustine found himself at the centre of a major controversy with the Pelagians over the nature of the human contribution to the act of salvation. So it was that the concern with the way of salvation, the place of faith, the meaning of repentance, the working of grace and the possibility of human preparation, for it came to dominate European theological thought for the greater part of its history. As it was from the genius of the Eastern Church that the most significant contributions to the classical Christological debate came, so it was from the Church in the West that Christian soteriological reflection received both its major direction and its deepest insights.

We now turn from the writings of one of the Church Fathers to a medieval work of Christian literature which takes up this idea of the Christian faith as a journey. It is significant for our study in that it illustrates the ongoing Western concern with eternal salvation and played a major role in shaping the way the popular mind reflected on the human predicament.

THE DIVINE COMEDY

Dante Alighieri (1265–1321) wrote his epic poem of a guided tour through the regions of hell, purgatory and heaven in the early fourteenth century. Like Augustine's *Confessions*, *The Divine Comedy* is generally recognized to be one of the great works of world literature. Its widespread influence throughout Italy led in due course to the standardization of the Italian language on the Tuscan dialect of its Florentine author. The form and purpose of the poem are somewhat similar to those of John Bunyan's *Pilgrim's Progress* in that an allegorical account of an individual's pilgrimage serves as a way of pointing the reader towards the path of salvation.

In the first section Dante is led by the spirit of Virgil, the classical poet, through each of the 24 great circles of Hell. The opening stanza introduces the principal allegory within which the narrative unfolds:

> Midway this way of life we're bound upon,
> I woke to find myself in a dark wood,
> Where the right road was wholly lost and gone.[5]

In mid-life the author discovers himself to be almost totally lost spiritually. His route back to God is one that must of necessity take him on an odyssey that starts with a tour of hell. It would appear that in order to receive divine grace, Dante needs to understand more clearly both the nature of sin and God's judgement on it. The leopard, lion and wolf that he encounters at the outset represent the principal temptations that confront the soul and can be more or less equated with lust, pride and envy. If these sins are not repented of, divine judgement will determine the soul's final inhabitation of one of the three corresponding divisions of hell.

The allegory is developed around a set of closely related theological ideas. First, the punishment meted out to the wrongdoer is both proportionate and appropriate to the nature of the determinative sin of his or her life. The author repeatedly uses the idea of poetic justice as a device to illustrate the seemliness of this relationship so that his readers can be assured that the divine sentence does indeed fit the crime. He intends their response to be similar to the approval they might give to a 'fair' judgement in a secular court of law. Secondly, hell, as the place of judgement, is a divine creation. On the gates of hell are written these words:

> Justice moved my great maker; God eternal
> Wrought me: the power and the unsearchably
> High wisdom, and the primal love supernal.[6]

The place of judgement is a creation of God, a work of his mysterious high wisdom. Although the inhabitants of hell might rage against their maker and live in eternal opposition to his rule and his person, all of its peoples and institutions are brought ultimately into his service. The apparent dualism between heaven and hell is thus modified by the final authority that God has over all his creation. Thirdly, and linked to both of these, Dante as our representative on this journey through the pathways of hell is called to affirm the goodness of the divine judgement in the face of the very natural desire to empathize with the misery of the sinner.

> Here pity, or here piety, must die
> If the other lives; who's wickeder than one
> That's agonized by God's high equity?[7]

We are called to side with piety rather than pity. The idea here is that it can only be our wickedness that makes us balk at the just judgement of God. The argument is not that every divine judgement is right simply because it is God who makes it and that it is our creaturely duty to align ourselves to his sovereign decision. Rather, Dante implies that there is a correspondence between the right action of God and our own sense of rightness and that when we are at our best we will recognize the goodness and appropriateness of all God's acts of judgement. It could not be otherwise for, as his readers were tacitly aware, the various punishments executed on the wicked in *The Divine Comedy* are not themselves derived directly from the scriptures or any other source of authority: they are but the constructs of the poet's own fertile imagination. Part of the artfulness in reading the poem then lies in assessing whether Dante, the author, has ordered the relative seriousness of various sins and their corresponding punishments as appropriately as Dante the pilgrim journeying through hell finds them to be. In making such assessment his readers are indirectly invited to share in the act of judgement against the celebrities of his age. But their participation in the process of judgement implies that they too are accountable citizens, responsible for their actions in a moral universe. For the ethical judgements we make on others clearly also apply to ourselves. Once we champion the need for fair judgement to be exercised so that the truth of a matter be disclosed and dealt with appropriately, we cannot with integrity expect to live outside of its orbit in a world where truth remains forever hidden.

What we have in *The Divine Comedy* is a medieval work of immense popularity and influence that took for granted the notion that we are accountable to God for our actions and that the outcome of his final judgement will be wholly appropriate to the way we have each lived. A serious consideration of these matters was held to be instrumental in receiving the grace and eternal salvation expounded in the later sections of the poem.

The third work we have chosen as a portal into the Western Church's view of the human predicament is a fresco in the Sistine Chapel, painted towards the end of the Italian Renaissance.

MICHELANGELO'S LAST JUDGEMENT

On 13 October 1534 the College of Cardinals elected Alessandro Farnese as bishop of Rome and spiritual leader of the Roman Catholic Church. Taking the name Pope Paul III he assumed the church's highest office at a turbulent and decisive period in its long history. The Protestant Reformation was gaining strength in the German and Swiss territories and it was becoming increasingly apparent that the church's institutions were in dire need of moral and theological reform. The Holy Roman Emperor, Charles V, the most influential secular ruler in Christendom, was demanding that an Ecumenical Council of the Church be convened to bring about a resolution of the crisis threatening the political stability of the region. Alongside these weighty ecclesial concerns the pope, as head of the Papal States, was also expected to act forcibly as a political and military leader advancing the temporal interests of the Church alongside those of his own family.

But the matter to which the new pope focused his immediate attention was of a quite different nature. Like a number of his predecessors Pope Paul III was a man with a highly developed artistic sensibility. It was a taste that had been cultivated during his studies in Florence in the heady days of Lorenzo the Magnificent under whose patronage the Italian Renaissance had flourished so spectacularly. It is then perhaps not wholly surprising that one of the first tasks to which Paul gave himself was the commissioning of a monumental work of religious art to distinguish his own papacy. He was determined to have a huge fresco of the Last Judgement painted on the altar wall of the papal chapel. He chose Michelangelo Buonarroti (1475–1564), the most celebrated artist of the day, for the project.

Notwithstanding his advanced age and all that he had already achieved in the world of art, Michelangelo gave himself tirelessly to this new papal project. After seven painstaking years *The Last Judgement* was finally completed. It is reported that when the pope first viewed the vast fresco he sank down on his knees in silent prayer. Before him, high above the altar, stood a stern and beardless Christ with his hand raised at the very instant of judgement. At his right side Mary lowers her eyes in humble submission, unable to play any part in the fateful decision that will determine the eternal fate of every human. Around Christ the eyes of the righteous look towards their judge with fear and trembling, awaiting his verdict. Below him with puffed-out cheeks angelic trumpeters blow with all their lungs, calling the dead to come forth from their graves. Hearing the trumpet blast their bones begin to take on flesh and sinews and angels graciously assist these newly constituted persons to rise upwards and heavenwards. Alongside them demons drag the unrighteous downwards to the netherworld. The classical figure of Charon forces these wretched persons into the barge that takes them across the Styx, the river of death, and drives them forward towards the gates of hell. One of the most unsettling images in the fresco is that of a number of the wicked attempting to force their way towards heaven but who find themselves being beaten back by determined angels with clenched fists.

Above the figure of Christ, angels can be seen carrying to heaven the emblems of his death including the cross, the crown of thorns, the nails and the pillar against which he was lashed. They, along with the marks of the crucifixion in his body, signify that the grace and mercy displayed in the justification of the faithful has been won through the suffering of the Son. Among the believers gathered around Jesus are a number of recognizable individuals each bearing witness to the triumph of grace. An elderly Peter who formerly disowned Jesus now carries in his hands the keys of the kingdom of heaven. Catherine is no longer fastened to the wheel on which she was martyred but holds a broken part of it as testimony of her final victory. Likewise, Sebastian flourishes the arrows by which he was slain and Bartholomew, who was flayed alive, carries at arm's length his own skin with a caricature on it of Michelangelo's face. What the artist is implying by introducing this self-depreciating signature is not certain. Possibly he reminds us that he is not a detached spectator of this final drama but that like all of us is required to be present personally before the judgement of Christ to wait for the final verdict on his own flawed life. Perhaps we catch here a glimpse of his hope that he too might be found somehow among those who are to be granted eternal life on the last day.

A painting of such dramatic intensity gives vivid expression to a particular theological world-view; what is in effect a carefully constructed belief-system about human destiny and accountability, the work of Christ and the nature of divine justice and saving grace. The question naturally arises: whose world are we peering into when we enter the Sistine Chapel and adjust our eyes to the light so that we can take in the scene before us? Is the fresco merely a door into the imaginative mind of a brilliant artist or do we have here a portrait of the shared theological vision of the contemporary church? Is this simply the presentation of one interpretation among many of our human outcome or does it faithfully encapsulate the dreadful uncertainty about individual destiny in the face of divine judgement that characterized so much of medieval religious consciousness?

There was certainly outrage among some members of the church hierarchy when *The Last Judgement* was first opened to public view. As it happened, this was not due to any theological concern about the painting, but because almost all of the figures were stark naked. Michelangelo had given the participants in this great moment of truth no external adornment to hide behind. It seemed that contemporary religious society in Rome found the nudity of the figures a far greater problem than any theology of judgement that the painting advanced. In due course drapery was introduced to cover over most of the offending bodily parts and the work was no longer considered offensive. Although the style and construction of the painting's themes were innovative, there was nothing novel about the theological ideas that lay behind them. Belief in the role of Christ as the final judge of all humankind had been shaped in the contemporary public mind by long-standing Christian tradition informed by the public reading of the scriptures and by popular works of Christian literature and art such as Dante's *The Divine Comedy.*

This would suggest that the Renaissance, with all its exuberant celebration of human possibilities, did little to undermine a vision of a world in which all are held accountable to God for the way they live. Rather, the political, social and theological turmoil threatening Florence and other Italian cities was being interpreted through the preaching of contemporaries like Savonarola as divine judgement against the widespread moral and religious decay of the Church and the perfidy of the political leaders. This is the world-view that informed Michelangelo and his fresco is a dramatic appeal both to the Church dignitaries and the wider public to reflect deeply on the matters of both divine condemnation and saving grace in the light of such a perspective.

Our fourth window into this Western interpretation of the human predicament in terms of sin and divine judgement is a twentieth-century relief sculpture by the French artist Auguste Rodin (1840–1917). As we will see it offers a rather different and more secular vista of the human plight.

RODIN'S GATES

In 1880 Rodin, fast gaining renown as a remarkable sculptor, was commissioned to fashion a bronze portal for the future museum of decorative arts in Paris. Inspired by Lorenzo Gibherti's bronze doors, *The Gates of Paradise*, on the Baptistry of St John's in Florence, Rodin chose as his subject *The Gates of Hell*. A number of the intended figures from this, his magnum opus, gained renown when they were later reworked as enlarged free-standing pieces.

Among them were *The Thinker, The Kiss, The Old Courtesan, The Prodigal, Fugit Amor, Ugolino, Eternal Springtime* and *Torso of a Young Woman.* These along with other components of the 'Gates' were repeatedly modified and repositioned as Rodin struggled over the years to do artistic justice to his awesome theme. When he died 37 years after the original commission, *The Gates of Hell* were still unfinished.

Rodin's portal is a dramatic visual interpretation of Dante's *Inferno*, the first section of *The Divine Comedy.* It is also deeply influenced by the artistic vision and style of Michelangelo. A swirling mass of doomed figures dance, leap and strive vainly for fulfilment as they are tormented by their own inner anguish. Some of their stories are known to us from Dante. Ugolino, the traitor of medieval Pisa, was imprisoned for his crime along with his sons. Legend has it that starving to death and driven to near insanity he devoured his own children. Rodin has positioned him on the lower section of the left door, groping blindly as he tries to grasp one of his offspring. Another cameo from *The Divine Comedy* that Rodin included in *The Gates* is the illicit love of Paolo Rimini for Francesca, his deformed brother's wife. Rising out of the right-hand door Paolo strives to hold on to Francesca who slips through his grasp in an eloquent portrayal of unattainable love. An earlier scene in their unfolding affair was captured in Rodin's depiction of them in a sensuous embrace which came to be known to the world simply as *The Kiss.* He later removed it from *The Gates*, sensing that its warmth detracted from the angst and hopelessness which his theme demanded. Above the doors, the three Shades point down to the writhing mass of lost souls below them. It is said that Rodin originally intended that the inscription on Dante's entrance into hell be included on his own *Gates*: 'Abandon all hope you who enter here.' And it was to these words that the Shades first gestured.

The principal feature of *The Gates* is the figure of Dante, possibly suggesting Rodin himself, deep in reflective thought, seated high in the centre of the Tympanum and looking out on all that is happening around him. His still, brooding, pensive outline serves as a counterpoint to the feverish, unfulfilled desires of the tormented souls below. The tragedy unfolding there serves as the cud for his own ruminations. We sense as we stand before this awesome scene that each of us is being invited to take upon ourselves the role of *The Thinker.*

What then are we to say of *The Gates of Hell*? What do they disclose of the Western perception of the human predicament? Clearly something has changed from the theological world-view that was shaped by Augustine and Dante and brought to visual expression by artists like Michelangelo. There is in *The Gates* no longer any suggestion of grace or hope. They speak only of overwhelming despair and frustrated desire. There is in them no allusion to the promise of redemption, to the work of Christ. In that sense they do not offer a Christian interpretation of judgement. Further, one senses as one considers their meaning that one has come to an age where the idea of hell as the place of divine judgement is a metaphor for our present predicament rather than a future eschatological reality. Rodin gives no indication that he is a religious man. The angst and despair of *The Gates of Hell* are tragic aspects of the human condition but they are not necessarily related to an authoritative decree of divine sentencing. There is no clear indication in the work that God is directly involved in this sea of anguish.

By the beginning of the twentieth century, the earlier understanding of the ordering of the cosmos had changed. Most Christians no longer felt comfortable in ascribing historical events of public or private suffering to an act of divine judgement. They just did not believe God would do such things. Nor did they generally consider a final day of reckoning to be a helpful focus for ordinary Christian reflection, even though they might officially subscribe to it as a dogma of the Church. For a number of reasons, not always easy to articulate, the act of judgement was considered to be appropriate for the civil courtroom, but not for the throne room of God. The understanding of human plight in the Western world had shifted. One might say it had become more secularized. Rodin's *Gates* suggest that our predicament has to do with our unrealized possibilities, our yearning for love, for freedom and for meaning, all of which can never be satisfied. In the twentieth century, partly influenced by Marxist analysis, the understanding of the human plight came to focus on the institutionalized social, economic and racial injustice that dehumanizes the lives of so many. Today, one of the most widely shared aspects of the way we perceive our plight is related to the threat that human greed brings to our planet as a safe place where life in all its fullness may flourish and be sustained. In all of these perspectives the act of divine judgement against sin has gradually but steadily shifted to the periphery of our interpretation of the problem that is before us. And as the perception of our plight has changed so too has the view of salvation which serves as solution to it. It is not easy within such a world-view to offer a persuasive explanation of how the death and resurrection of Christ resolves these issues.

I have suggested that if we are to understand how the doctrine of justification functioned historically as a theory of salvation we need to appreciate the context in which it flourished. I have argued that over a considerable period Western Christian thought interpreted our predicament in terms of human sin and divine judgement and I have illustrated this by briefly considering some of its leading works of literature and art. It is into this possibly strange world that we need to enter imaginatively if we are to do justice to our subject-matter.

Before proceeding to a study of justification within this perspective, one further question remains. What are we to make of this interpretation of the human predicament that held sway over so many Western Christian minds until modern times? Few Christians today would view Michelangelo's representation of Christ with his arm raised in judgement as an appropriate expression of God's response to humankind. It appears to undermine radically his goodness, his love and his mercy. Of course, theologians of those times would look on our present disinclination to affirm God's judgement against sin or to uphold human accountability before him as an attitude that lies close to blasphemy.

If we are to move forward in making an assessment of former perspectives, perhaps the most fruitful question we can consider is: 'How Christian was the earlier Western concern with human sin and divine judgement?' How well does it reflect the emphasis of the scriptures and in particular that of the New Testament? How harmonious is it with the teaching of Jesus? And it is with questions such as these in mind that we turn to the New Testament documents.

CHAPTER 2

DIVINE JUDGEMENT IN THE NEW TESTAMENT

In the chapters which follow we shall see how the doctrine of justifi-cation was developed and modified in the West within a world-view dominated by an understanding of the human predicament in terms of sin and divine judgement. But first it would be helpful to assess whether there is in fact a broad biblical basis for such an under-standing of our plight. For example, does the grand vision of the 'Last Day', that we find so graphically portrayed in Michelangelo's Last Judgement, actually reflect the context in which the gospel is presented in the New Testament?

It was suggested in the previous chapter that modern Christian consciousness has moved some distance away from Michelangelo's perspective, and that it is not easy for Christians today to align themselves with a Christ who has his hand raised in a dreadful act of final judgement. Many would argue that God's redemptive action through his Son has effectively dealt with the matter of con-demnation for sin and that to focus our attention on divine judge-ment would require us to overlook both the unbounded love of God as well as the consequences of the atoning work of Christ.

We need to reflect on these concerns for a moment, for they take us right to the heart of the matter. Justification, in its clas-sical expression, is the way in which God, acting through his Son and Spirit, resolves the predicament that has arisen through sin and judgement. If this is the case, an outline of the depth of our plight might well throw light on the nature of the gospel that rescues us from it. In short, to focus our attention on the idea of divine judge-ment need not of itself be a morbid exercise in misanthropy, but can rather highlight the divine graciousness displayed in Jesus. Like

Augustine's fearless moral audit, a study of the concept of judgement may yet enlarge our appreciation of the love of God. To reiterate an earlier argument: the study of the cure is closely related to an understanding of the disease.

We return then to our original question: Is the view of sin, alienation and divine judgement that gave shape to Western Christianity's understanding of the human predicament firmly rooted in the scriptures? Leaving aside, for the moment, other themes let us consider briefly the text of the New Testament and in particular its presentation of the teaching of Jesus to see what they have to say about final judgement.

PARABLES OF THE KINGDOM

There is something rather enigmatic about the nature of kingdom of heaven that was proclaimed by the young rabbi from Galilee. It is not easy to be certain whether he was claiming that the kingdom was already present in his ministry or was something that still lay in the future; whether it was internal to the believer and, therefore, hidden and needing discovery or a public and external reality obvious to all; whether it had political and social dimensions that touched the wider world or was narrowly religious and affected only the people of faith. Perhaps it is because of its somewhat mysterious character that Jesus often used parables to explain it. The kingdom of heaven seems to be a truth that only those with 'ears to hear' can properly understand. There is, however, one particular feature of the kingdom that appears to be remarkably clear. And it is this aspect we will now examine. In doing so, we will, at least initially, limit ourselves to a consideration of the words of Jesus as we find them recorded in Matthew's Gospel.

Jesus likened the coming kingdom of heaven to a man who sowed good seed in his field, but an enemy came after him and sowed weeds among the wheat (Mt. 13.24-30). The servants of the landowner were eager to pull up the weeds, but he ordered them to allow both weeds and wheat to grow together until the harvest. Jesus went on to explain what the parable meant: 'As the weeds are pulled up and burned in the fire, so it will be at the end of the age. The Son of Man will send his angels, and they will weed out of his kingdom everything that causes sin and all who do evil' (Mt. 13.41).

18

Likewise Jesus taught that the kingdom of heaven can be compared to a net that caught all kinds of fish. When it was full the fishermen collected the good fish in baskets, but threw the bad away. Again he explains the parable. 'This is how it will be at the end of the age. The angels will come and separate the wicked from the righteous' (Mt. 13.49). It would appear from these parables that the kingdom of heaven has to do with an act of judgement, a separation of those who do evil, from those who are righteous.

Jesus promised his disciples that: 'When the Son of Man comes in his glory, and all the angels with him, he will sit on his glorious throne. All the nations will be gathered before him, and he will separate the people one from another, as a shepherd separates the sheep from the goats' (Mt. 25.31). The same basic idea that we found in the previous two sayings is repeated here, but the basis of the judgement is rather more explicit. It has to do with how those now standing before his throne in judgement treated the brothers and sisters of Jesus when they found them naked, thirsty or in prison. The idea is spelled out a little more clearly earlier in the Gospel.

Anyone who welcomes you welcomes me, and anyone who welcomes me welcomes the one who sent me . . . And if anyone gives even a cup of cold water to one of these little ones who is my disciple, truly I tell you, that person will certainly be rewarded. (Mt. 10.40, 42)

The parable of the wedding banquet (Mt. 22.1-14) develops this emphasis on the eternal significance of our actions and focuses on the way we respond to the gospel. Jesus speaks of the destruction that will be brought on those on the guest list who, for a variety of reasons, refused the king's invitation to his son's wedding. It also emphasizes the king's judgement against the man who attended the celebration improperly dressed. We find then that for Jesus the kingdom of heaven is not merely an act of separation of the good from the wicked, but takes the form of an authoritative judgement, rewarding those who have behaved in an appropriate way and punishing those who have not.

Also to be found in Matthew's Gospel is a set of parables that refer to the way the Lord will deal with his servants who have been idle while their master is absent and who are consequently ill-prepared for his return. The parable of the talents (Mt. 25.14-28) tells of the reward that was given to those who faithfully employed what was entrusted to them and the punishment that befell the man who failed to use what had been placed in his care. The parable of the virgins (Mt. 25.1-13) promises exclusion to those who are not properly prepared for the bridegroom's return. The parable of the tenants (Mt. 21.33-45) indicates that there will be a fearful end for those who did not offer the fruit of the vineyard to their rightful master, but abused his servants and murdered his son. All these, Jesus explains to his followers, indicate what the kingdom is like. It is reward for those who faithfully serve God in preparation for his Son's return, but it is punishment for those who abuse the steward-ship that has been assigned to them. Again we see that the kingdom of heaven is conceived of by Jesus as an event whose principal fea-ture is an act of divine judgement.

In all these sayings the Kingdom of God corresponds closely to the expression 'the day of the Lord' found in the Old Testament prophetic expectation. This is uniformly anticipated to be a day of divine judgement, leading either to destruction or to salvation (see Isa. 2.17; Joel 1.15; Isa. 25.9). One might say it is a day of final decision.

Multitudes, multitudes in the valley of decision!

For the day of the Lord is near in the valley of decision. (Joel 3.14)

The coming of the kingdom is understood as a time when the divine government of the one true king will be manifest on earth, the people of God will be vindicated openly and the unrighteous condemned.

CONFESSION AND BAPTISM

Now if at the heart of the message of the kingdom lies the idea of divine judgement, did those who heard it proclaimed publicly recognize it as such? We catch a glimpse of the common under-standing of the kingdom in the way many responded to the min-istry of John the Baptist. Like Jesus, John announced the coming kingdom of heaven. His words in Matthew's Gospel take much the same form as those of Jesus recorded in Mark's Gospel. 'In those days John the Baptist came, preaching in the wilderness of Judea and saying, "Repent for the kingdom of heaven has come near"'

(Mt. 3.1, 2). The result of John's preaching, as we have it in the scriptures, was that multitudes came down from Jerusalem, Judea and the whole region of the Jordan to be baptized by John on confession of their sins. It was as though an amnesty had been declared and vast crowds of concerned Judeans hurriedly made their way down to the Jordan River to take up this offer of grace before it was too late. So it was that when John saw a group of Pharisees jostling their way towards him through the throng, he said to them: 'You brood of vipers! Who warned you to flee from the coming wrath?' (v. 7). For one reason or another John was surprised to see these Pharisees join with the ordinary folk in their flight from the coming judgement. He warns them of its imminence: 'The axe is already at the root of the trees and every tree that does not produce good fruit will be cut down and thrown into the fire' (v. 10). This theme of impending judgement is also present in the way John goes on to describe the ministry of Jesus. 'He will baptize you with the Holy Spirit and with fire. His winnowing fork is in his hand, and he will clear his threshing floor, gathering his wheat into the barn and burning up the chaff with unquenchable fire' (vv. 11, 12). The message of John is remarkably similar to Jesus' parable of the weeds. Judgement is a key feature of the proclamation of the kingdom and it is in the expectation of this divine judgement that the people confessed their sins and received the cleansing water of baptism.

WARNING AGAINST SIN

Jesus, like John, was deeply concerned with certain ways of behaving that he encountered in his public ministry and he sternly warned those practising them of the reality of final judgement. One of these had to do with the treatment of children. 'If anyone causes one of these little ones – those believing in me – to stumble, it would be better for them if a large millstone were hung around their neck and they were drowned in the depths of the sea' (Mt. 18.6). There is a sense of righteous anger behind these words that it is easy for us to identify with as we hear of so many of the children of our own day being 'groomed' on the internet. The warning would seem to apply, however, to all those knowing adults who lead impressionable youngsters away from the path of truth. Another major concern of Jesus was with those who profess faith but who fail to forgive those who are in some way indebted to them. In the parable of the unmerciful servant (Mt. 18.21-35) the one who had been set free from a great debt was unable to forgive his fellow servant for what was in effect no more than a small loan. On finding out what had happened the master orders the unmerciful servant to undergo terrible punishment until he should repay his original obligation. Jesus concludes: 'This is how my heavenly Father will treat each of you unless you forgive a brother or sister from your heart' (v. 35).

Although sins like these can be considered as personal or individual, Jesus also responds to what we now sometimes refer to as corporate sin, a behavioural pattern that is embedded in the life of a community. Although he had a number of friends among the Pharisees, they as a group are the subject of his most severe words of condemnation (Mt. 23.1-36). In the eyes of Jesus the principal darkness that stains the lives of this party of religious elite is their hypocrisy. It can be observed in their love for religious dress; in the way they strive for positions of religious honour and in their desire to be addressed by their religious titles. It is all about outward appearance (vv. 5-7). The Pharisees were scrupulous over the external details of the law, but continually missed the heart of the matter (vv. 23-24). Outwardly they appeared to be righteous, inwardly they were full of hypocrisy and wickedness. Jesus says of them: 'You brood of vipers. How will you escape being condemned to hell?' (v. 33).

We see then that the prospect of final judgement is employed by Jesus as a dire warning to those caught up in ways of behaving that undermine both the truth and practice of the gospel. Although his words are uncompromising, he is not displaying the vindictiveness of a moral legalist. Rather, out of deep love and a desire for integrity he is drawing attention to issues that really do matter the abuse of children; the heartless and unforgiving treatment of those who are in our debt; and the overweening sense of self-importance and hypocrisy of the clerical classes. Behind his warnings lies the conviction that God is not so unjust as to turn a blind eye to such ways of behaving but will hold to full account all those who participate in them.

THE AGENT OF JUDGEMENT

An important feature of the New Testament emphasis on divine judgement is that the ascended Christ is recognized as its principal agent. Jesus, the one who had shared fully in our humanity and had given himself up for our sins will return as our judge. In Matthew's Gospel Jesus is reported as saying: 'For the Son of Man is going to come in his Father's glory with his angels, and then he will reward everyone according to what they have done' (Mt. 16.27). He taught that it is the Son of Man who will judge the sheep and the goats (Mt. 25.31). Likewise it is the Son of Man who will send his angels to weed out of his kingdom everything that causes sin and all who do evil (Mt. 13.41).

Peter's sermon on the Day of Pentecost, as we find it in the Acts of the Apostles, gives some indication of how Jesus began to be viewed by his followers with a new sense of awe after his ascension. When the assembled crowd heard that he had been raised from the dead and exalted to a position of authority at the right hand of God they were cut to the heart and were desperate to know what they should now do (Acts 2.36, 37). Recognizing the implications of his divinely appointed status of authority they repented of their sins and were baptized.

This understanding of Jesus as the plenipotentiary of God who will return to judge the living and the dead was an integral feature of the faith of the New Testament church. It is to be found not only in the Gospels, but across the Epistles (see 2 Cor. 5.10; 2 Thess. 1.7-8), and most graphically in the book of Revelation where Jesus leads an army of horsemen clad in white to execute the judgement of God (Rev. 19.11-16). The theme of the Son of Man as judge on the Last Day is perhaps the clearest indication we have of the way the idea of final judgement shaped the world-view of New Testament thought.

In our brief study of the text of Matthew's Gospel we have seen that final judgement was an integral element of the coming kingdom of heaven; that it was a principal motivation for multitudes who heard of it to be baptized; that it was repeatedly used by Jesus to warn of the consequence of certain forms of behaviour; and finally that it is the role assigned to the risen and ascended Christ as he returns in glory. To the question: 'Is the broad theological vision of a final judgement that was so dramatically portrayed in Michelangelo's Last Judgement firmly based on the teaching and preaching of the New Testament?' the answer would, of course, have to be 'yes'. The world-view of the Western Church informed by the ideas of sin and judgement, which was outlined in the previous chapter and which extended from Augustine to well after Michelangelo, is in basic harmony with the message of the scriptures and is in that sense thoroughly Christian.

How does all this relate to the doctrine of justification? I have argued that there is a close relation between the ideas of sin and judgement and the doctrine of justification as it developed in the West. So far, through a brief survey of some significant works of literature and art, I have offered a sketch of how these ideas were both perceived and developed within Western religious consciousness. We have also seen in this chapter that this understanding is broadly based on biblical testimony. But in order to link this view of the human plight with the concept of justification we will need to demonstrate that there is a clear relationship between the ideas of sin and judgement and that of justification in Paul's exposition of the subject. We do so by briefly examining the text of his letter to the Romans.

JUDGEMENT IN ROMANS

The letter to the Romans takes the form of a treatise, that is, it exhibits a carefully developed argument, along with a number of explanatory branches. One becomes aware of this structure as one reads the letter, for each section appears either to flow from something that went before or to raise questions that are soon to be addressed. So it is that the passage (1.18–3.20) that begins with the phrase 'The wrath of God is being revealed from heaven against all the godlessness and wickedness of human beings' and concludes with the sentence 'Therefore no one will be declared righteous in God's sight' not only develops a single theme, but lays a foundation for what is to follow. One might say that it poses a problem that is in urgent need of resolution.

What then is the theme of the passage that finds its place between the introduction of the idea of the 'righteousness of God' as the essence of the gospel (1.17) and expounds it as the justification of sinners (3.21–5.21)? It has to do with divine judgement. Paul argues that each of the various communities in which he finds himself, whether pagan libertines, morally earnest Greeks or the community of Jews, lie under the condemning judgement of God. The expression the 'wrath of God is being revealed' with which the passage opens can be taken as being broadly synonymous with the phrase

'God's condemning judgement is apparent'. We saw above in the parables of the kingdom that the concept of judgement involves an act of separation, whereby some are condemned and punished while others are justified and rewarded. In this passage the emphasis is on the divine censure.

First, Paul argues that the pagans 'suppress the truth by their wickedness' and have 'exchanged the glory of the immortal God for images' (1.18). But, he maintains, they do this in the face of the clear revelation that God has given of himself in creation. For the created world in all its manifold wonder is a public manifestation of God's 'eternal power and divine nature'. These aspects of his nature 'have been clearly seen, being understood from what has been made, so that people are without excuse' (1.20). Although they had a knowledge of God, they did not give him the honour that was his due, but instead chose to debase themselves and worship the images of creatures. We find here a key notion that underlines the argument of the whole section. 'They are all without excuse.' The condemning judgement to which Paul refers is made on the grounds that each person understands aspects of the truth about God, but has turned away from this light, thereby denying him the glory that is his due. It means that those behaving in such a way will not be able to justify their actions before God. No defence can be offered for their creature-centred forms of worship.

It is interesting that Paul views the licentiousness of the pagans not as the reason for divine condemnation, but as an indication that they already lie under it. 'Therefore God gave them over in the sinful desires of their hearts to sexual impurity' (1.24). The removal of moral restraints, the collapse of social norms of right behaviour is itself a sign of God's censure. To gain some insight into Paul's view of pagan practice in the first century, one might consider the Moslem perception of current Western moral decadence. The widespread availability of pornography, the open abuse of alcohol and drugs, the public display of nudity, the glamorization of infidelity on the screens of cinema and television, the breakdown of family cohesion and the erosion of respect for authority all suggest to the Islamic mind that God has long since given up on the greater part of Western society. He appears to have withdrawn his gracious hand of restraint. It might well be that the Islamic perception of the West gives us a glimpse of the way Paul and other conscientious Jews felt about aspects of the pagan world of their own day.

JUSTIFICATION: A GUIDE FOR THE PERPLEXED

Second, an articulate moral subculture flourished within the Graeco-Roman world that Paul inhabited. There were those around him, guided by the writings of the philosophers or even by their own personal principles of common decency, who sought in their lives to do what was right. They would no doubt have been highly critical of the moral laxity so apparent in the public life of Roman society. Paul turns his attention to their particular predicament:

> You, therefore, have no excuse, you who pass judgement on someone else, for at whatever point you judge another, you are condemning yourself, because you who pass judgement do the same thing. (Rom. 2.1)

The ethical system which is presupposed in our condemnation of others becomes the basis on which we ourselves are to be judged. And Paul's point is that we universally fail to live up to the measure by which we hold others accountable. It means that self-assured moralists, who are acutely aware of the licentiousness and sexual perversity of their neighbours but who are stubbornly unwilling to recognize their own failings, are in a precarious position with God.

> But because of your stubbornness and your unrepentant heart, you are storing up wrath against yourself for the day of God's wrath, when his righteous judgement will be revealed. God will repay everyone according to what they have done. (2.5-6)

Religious affiliation is of no help here, '[f]or God does not show favouritism' (2.11). The Jews will be judged by the law that has been given to them by Moses. The pagans will be judged by the subjective laws which determine their own ethical practice. Depending on the way they have lived each will receive either eternal life or condemning judgement. 'This will take place on the day when God judges everyone's secrets through Jesus Christ' (2.16). The same underlying principle as the one to which we drew attention above is stressed. Those who find themselves under divine condemnation will have no excuse (2.1). Their own consciences testify that what they are doing is wrong, otherwise they would not have so readily condemned their neighbours. And consequently they are rightly held to account for their actions.

Third, Paul turns to his own community, the Jews. The Jews understood themselves as a chosen nation, a people who had been adopted into the family of the one true God and who now lived in holy covenant with him. Through the Torah they knew the divine will and were called to exhibit to the world the truth about God and his ways. The sad reality, however, was that they were not fulfilling this high calling, but had rather brought dishonour to the name of the God they served. It is rather like what happens today when the Church abuses in its institutions the very children it has promised to protect. We can catch a sense of the indignation in Paul's words:

> [Y]ou, then, who teach others, do you not teach yourself? You who preach against stealing, do you steal? You who say that people should not commit adultery, do you commit adultery? You who abhor idols, do you rob temples? You who boast in the law, do you dishonour God by breaking the law? As it is written, God's name is blasphemed among the Gentiles because of you. (2.21-24)

Now if the Jews also lie under divine condemnation, the obvious question arises: 'What advantage then, is there in being a Jew?' (3.1). The response Paul gives need not divert us here. The point is that he has described a scenario of divine judgement which demands that such a question be addressed.

Paul summarizes his exposition of the predicament into which each of these communities find themselves (3.9-20). All of them both Jews and Gentiles are trapped under the power of sin. He offers an array of scriptures to support his thesis that there is no exception to this pessimistic conclusion. 'There is no one righteous, not even one' (3.10). The argument of the section is brought to a head in its final two verses:

> Now we know that whatever the law says, it says to those who are under the law, so that every mouth may be silenced and the whole world held accountable to God. Therefore no one will be declared righteous in God's sight by observing the law, rather, through the law comes the knowledge of sin. (3.19, 20)

The defence is silent because in the face of all the evidence that has been marshalled there is no longer anything left to say. Judged

27

by the standards of the law, external or internal, nobody will be justified by God. Here, in essence, is the human predicament.

This section of Paul's letter to the Romans indicates that the concepts of sin and divine judgement not only shape the New Testament world-view as we have seen in the recorded teaching of Jesus but provide the immediate context for Paul's exposition of the concept of justification. It carefully details the nature of a plight so serious that there can be no human escape from it. Only God can provide a way out. Broadly speaking, the doctrine of justification is an account of how God has resolved the human predicament understood in terms of sin and divine judgement. It is, in short, an explanation of how God justifies the ungodly.

SUMMARY

A parable might be the best way to remind ourselves of the route we have taken in the previous two chapters. I am standing before a bronze cast of Rodin's Thinker outside the National Museum of Western Art in central Tokyo. A group of young Japanese students touring the gallery recognize me as a Westerner and ask me if I can explain the sculpture. We don't seem to be pressed for time and they appear to be interested, so I tell them a story. I tell them of Jesus of Nazareth, a man from God who spoke of a coming kingdom where everyone would be one day divided into one of two groups, sheep or goats, for divine condemnation or justification. I introduce them to the great African bishop Augustine who having chosen to follow Jesus reflected deeply on the nature of his sins. I encourage them to walk with the Italian poet Dante on a journey through hell in the hope that he might attain heaven. I paint for them mental pictures of Michelangelo's Last Judgement fresco in the Sistine Chapel and of Rodin's Gates of Hell and the swirling mass of despairing figures that constituted it. Only now do we turn to thoughtful gaze of Rodin's thinker. 'What do you think is on that man's mind?' I ask them. After a period of reflective silence one particularly perceptive student replies: 'The sort of things you have been talking about.' And with that insight she has perhaps come closer than many professional art critics to understand what this pensive, brooding figure is all about.

The context in which 'The Thinker' is best understood is the setting in which Rodin fashioned him – high on the Tympanum, gazing down on the swirling mass of writhing bodies unable to escape their personal frustration, guilt and torment. So too, the classical doctrine of justification can only be interpreted aright within its own context. It is good news for those who find themselves standing silent in the dock, convicted by divine law, and aware that they stand guilty before God, deserving of his condemning judgement.

Having painted in the backdrop let us turn our attention to the leading actors on the stage and learn from their discussion how the doctrine of justification was developed in the Western Church. We begin with Augustine of Hippo who might well have possessed the most formative mind the post-apostolic Christian Church has yet produced.

CHAPTER 3

AUGUSTINE OF HIPPO

Paul argued in a letter he wrote to the Christians in Rome that everyone, both Jews and Gentiles, is being held to solemn account before God. He maintained that in the face of the charges that the law brings against them no one is able to offer a persuasive defence for what they have done. Their deeds have been brought to light in the divine presence and everyone is now appropriately silent, unable to present any excuse for their wrongdoings. It is in the setting of what we might call the Supreme Court and in the expectation of a ruling from its high judge that Paul makes a dramatic announcement of good news. A justifying judgement, which he describes as the righteousness of God, has been made public. It is a judgement in favour of the ungodly, not through their fulfilment of the law's requirements, but through their faith in Jesus Christ and on the basis of all that has been accomplished in his life, death and resurrection.

Within this rich network of ideas lies the essence of the Christian doctrine of justification. The promise of salvation outlined here appears to be simple and straight forward. Yet explaining what its principal concepts, including those of law, faith, justification and the righteousness of God, mean in this context has long been a matter of vigorous debate among Christians. One might say that the doctrine of justification is the ongoing attempt of the Church to offer a coherent account of this summary statement of salvation, or one similar to it, in the framework of all that it believes to be true.

The task before us is to explore how this doctrine was understood and developed in the Western Church. Although we will consider the work of only a comparatively small number of leading theologians, I trust that they will provide us with a fair sketch of the way the Church has grappled with the issues. The survey of their thought and critical engagement with it is not itself the goal of this study but is intended rather to serve as a tool. The intention is to come to a clearer perception of what Paul himself intended in his use of the concept and so make sense of the profound promise in the scriptures that God justifies the ungodly through their faith in Jesus. We begin with a study of the work of Aurelius Augustinus, bishop of Hippo.

The influence of Augustine on Western Christian thought has been immense. This is due in part to his penetrating spiritual insight and the clarity of his theological reasoning. But his abiding influence is also related to the high esteem in which he came to be held by the wider Christian community, particularly after his notable triumph in the Pelagian debate. As a result, some of his theological ideas came to be accepted as authoritative within the Western Church simply because they were his. It makes a critical examination of his work particularly important. Let us look at how he interpreted the concept of justification and the group of ideas relating to it.

THE HUMAN PREDICAMENT

Augustine held that humans entered into their present troubled condition when God first gave them his law. Using the free-will with which they were created, our first parents chose to disobey God's command. The consequence of their action was that they found themselves guilty before him with a free-will that had become bound or crippled by sin. In short, they no longer had the power within themselves to make good choices. As their offspring, we now all share both in their guilt and their natural inability to act rightly or choose properly. Further, sin has come to dominate our lives, strengthened as it is by the stringent demands of the law. The paradox is that the harder we try to do what is right, the more we find ourselves trapped in sin's potent grasp.

Afterwards, when through the law has come the knowledge of sin, and the Spirit of God has not yet interposed His aid, man, striving to live according to the law, is thwarted in his efforts and falls into conscious sin, and so, being overcome of sin, becomes its slave. (*The Enchiridion*, 118)[1]

We are, argues Augustine, accountable to God for the wrong that we do and will be judged with a severity which is proportional to our disobedience. '[T]he punishment of each will be more tolerable in the next world, according as his iniquity has been less in this world' (*The Enchiridion*, 93).[2]

According to Augustine there are four aspects to our present human predicament: shared guilt and with it death, the bondage of our free-will, the domination of our lives by the principle of sin and the dreadful prospect of divine judgement for the evil we have done. Salvation or justification, which is a closely related idea in Augustine's thought, is God's remedy for the fourfold difficulty in which we find ourselves.

THE WORK OF CHRIST

Augustine believed that our salvation is founded on the saving work of Jesus Christ. While most of his contemporaries interpreted Jesus' death in terms of a ransom paid to the devil or as a means that God used to deceive him, Augustine, held that Christ overcame Satan's hold on us by defeating him through his righteous death and powerful resurrection.[3] However, Augustine's particular emphasis in his interpretation of the atonement was on Christ's role as a mediator between humankind and God. Augustine was aware that if our alienation from the Father is the most urgent problem facing us we are in dire need of a mediator, someone who is able to stand between us and God and reconcile us to him. His preferred concept for explaining this reconciling or mediatorial work of Christ was the idea of sacrifice. Augustine showed a remarkable awareness of the complexity of the issues involved when Jesus' death was viewed in this way:

> In such wise that, whereas four things are to be considered in every sacrifice, – to whom it is offered, by whom it is offered, what is offered, for whom it is offered, – the same one and true Mediator Himself, reconciling us to God by the sacrifice of peace, might remain one with Him to whom He offered, might make those one in Himself for whom he offered, Himself might be in one both the offerer and the offering. (*The Trinity*, 4.19)[4]

Students of Augustine generally find themselves, at some point, referring to this Father of the Catholic Church as a genius. I confess that after unpacking this convoluted sentence and considering its various components I cannot recall having come across a summary theological statement which so concisely holds together the central Christian truths regarding salvation, the person of Christ and the Church.

Although Augustine affirms Christ's divine status, he recognizes that the mediatorial work of Christ is actually accomplished by him as man.

> He is the Mediator between God and men, Jesus Christ, who is a man, and he appeared on earth between men, who are sinful and mortal, and God, who is immortal and just. Like men he was mortal: like God, he was just . . . For as man, he is our Mediator; but as the Word of God, he is not an intermediary between God and man because he is equal with God, and God with God, and together with him one God. (*Confessions*, 10.43)[5]

Jesus as Mediator was human in every way just as we are, yet he remained without sin. Augustine interprets 'God made him who had no sin to be sin' (2 Cor. 5.21) not as 'Jesus became sinful, or was made sinful' but rather: 'on account of the likeness of sinful flesh in which He came, He was called sin, that he might wash away sin . . . He, then, being made sin, just as we are made righteousness (our righteousness being not our own, but God's, not in ourselves but in Him' (*The Enchiridion*, 41).[6] We must be particularly careful in our reading of Augustine here. Although this righteousness of the believer seems to be very much like the alien righteousness so central to Luther's exposition, which we will examine later, it would appear that Augustine's understanding of the nature of the righteousness of a justified Christian is in fact somewhat different from that of the German Reformer.

THE RIGHTEOUSNESS OF THE JUSTIFIED

What does it mean, according to Augustine, to be justified, to be made righteous? The following passage offers an insight into his understanding of the life of the justified sinner. Augustine has been speaking of the one who is trapped by the power of sin and frustrated in his attempts to do what the law requires.

> But if God has regard to him, and inspires him with faith in God's help, and the Spirit of God begins to work in him, then the mightier power of love strives against the power of the flesh; and although there is still in the man's own nature a power that fights against him . . . yet he lives the life of the just by faith, and lives in righteousness so far as he does not yield to evil lust, but conquers it by the love of holiness. (*The Enchiridion*, 118)[7]

Those justified by faith are empowered in the midst of great turmoil and inner conflict to live a life of righteousness, a life that does not give in to temptation but loves the way of holiness. Augustine understands Jesus' words in Matthew's Gospel 'do not do your acts of righteousness in front of others' as indicating the shape that a righteous life might take. It has to do with day-to-day Christian spirituality, including private prayer, secret almsgiving and unnoticed fasting. These are its outward forms, but Augustine argues that the life of a person who has been made righteous by faith is a spiritual journey that is directed continually by a God-given loving attitude:

> Our righteousness in this pilgrimage is this – that we press forward to the perfect and full righteousness in which there shall be perfect and full love in the sight of his glory; and that now we hold to the rectitude and perfection of our course. (*On Man's Perfection in Righteousness*, 18)[8]

Justification is the act of God that brings about this way of righteous living, it makes us righteous. To anticipate later discussions justification forms in us a created rather than an imputed righteousness. There is, however, no suggestion in Augustine that it is a pattern of life that we are able to establish for ourselves. The converse is true. This new righteousness is wholly dependent on God's empowering. Only by God's gracious working in our lives we are able to be righteous.

> [S]o also man, even when most fully justified, is unable to lead a holy life, if he be not divinely assisted by the eternal light of

righteousness. God, therefore, heals us not only that He may blot out the sin which we have committed, but, furthermore, that He may enable us even to avoid sinning. (*On Nature and Grace*, 29)[9]

When Augustine speaks of our righteousness being not our own but God's, he is indicating that God is the author of this transformation of our lives. It is not something that we can of ourselves manufacture. Justification is for him not only an act of pardon but the creation of a new way of living. This formation of righteousness in a person is always viewed by Augustine as an ongoing process rather than an instantaneous, completed act.

But, it might be asked, are not the lives of some pagans more righteous than many of those who have been justified? Augustine concedes that outwardly it appears to be the case. However, righteousness is not understood by him merely as the external fulfilment of the law's demands. It is about the heart; it has to do with motivation; ultimately it is about love. If the 'commandment is kept from the fear of punishment and not from the love of righteousness, it is servilely kept, not freely, and therefore it is not kept at all. For no fruit is good which does not grow from the root of love' (*On the Spirit and the Letter*, 26).[10] Augustine views the obedience that is motivated by a fear of the law rather than by love as a circumcision of the flesh and not of the heart. It is wholly different from the righteousness of the justified. It certainly carries no weight with God.

We see then that Augustine interprets 'to justify' as meaning 'to make righteous in behaviour'. That God justifies the ungodly is not for him a paradoxical statement. It simply means that God enables those who are unrighteous to start living and acting righteously. Alister McGrath suggests that although this is a permissible reading of the Latin word 'justificare', it is an unacceptable rendering of the Hebrew concept underlying it.[11] To try and understand the significance of his concern, consider the outcome of other judicial decisions such as 'pardon', 'vindicate', 'exonerate' and 'acquit'. Actions such as these might affect someone's relationships or status but not necessarily their person or habits. Now if this is how the verb 'to justify' was used in Paul's letters, it might be that Augustine's understanding of the word has somewhat confused our reading of the apostle. It is a matter to which we will need to return in due course. For now, however, let us turn our attention to his understanding of the human part in this justifying action of God.

JUSTIFYING FAITH

Augustine argued that salvation is to be attained not as a reward for good works nor by a free decision of the will, but through the gracious gift of faith (*The Enchiridion*, 30). For those who have not received divine grace are unable to do good works or achieve anything that is acceptable to God by their own free choice. The reason is that the human will is no longer free. It is in bondage to sin.

However, the nature of the faith through which a person is justified needs to be considered carefully. Even the devils believe and faith such as theirs is clearly of no advantage to them. Justifying faith is for Augustine a particular way of believing, it is a faith that works through love: 'the faith which saves us is that which the Apostle Paul clearly enough describes when he says: "For in Jesus Christ neither circumcision availeth anything, nor uncircumcision, but faith which worketh by love"' (*The Enchiridion*, 67).[12] Saving faith is for Augustine a faith characterized by the practice of loving action. It means that those who persevere in wrongdoing and do not exhibit love in their relation to others can take no comfort from their belief in Christ.

In Augustine's view, love is the determining characteristic of the Christian life. It is the one distinguishing feature of those who will receive eternal salvation.

> There is no gift of God more excellent than this. It alone distinguishes the sons of the eternal kingdom and the sons of eternal perdition. Other gifts, too, are given by the Holy Spirit; but without love they profit nothing. (*On the Trinity*, 15.32)[13]

On occasion Augustine identifies love with the external act of charity or giving to the poor. And so it is that almsgiving itself becomes, in his view, a means of attaining salvation or pardon. He finds this idea in Jesus' words to the Pharisees: 'Give alms of such things as you have; and, behold, all things are clean unto you' (*The Enchiridion*, 75, p. 261). He also emphasizes that care for those in need is the principle by which God will separate the righteous from the unrighteous on the day of final judgement (Mt. 25.31-46). Referring to love Augustine writes: 'How great a good, then, without which goods so great bring no one eternal life!' (*On the Trinity*, 15.18, p. 217). This understanding of the saving nature of charitable action is apparent in his pastoral direction to erring believers that 'almsgiving must be used to propitiate God for past sins' (*The Enchiridion*, 70, p. 260).

When Augustine argues that the lost cannot be redeemed through their good works, it is not because he believes that such works are not meritorious, but rather that those who have not been born anew are simply unable to perform them. Good works are in fact worthy of reward for those who have been justified. Eternal life is the recompense due to them. But, as Augustine continuously emphasized, all these works are no more than the gracious action of God in us.

> We are to understand, then, that man's good deserts are themselves the gift of God, so that when these obtain the recompense of eternal life, it is simply grace given for grace. (*The Enchiridion*, 107, p. 271)

In Augustine's thought 'faith working through love' is both the human virtue through which justification is received and the essential feature of the righteousness which justification brings about. There is consequently no dichotomy in his thought between salvation through good works and salvation through faith, for these gracious gifts of God are in effect two sides of the same coin. Rather, the radical disjunction in the way we view our role in salvation, according to Augustine, is whether we understand it in terms of an action of our own nature or whether we see it is as a work of grace.

GRACE

Augustine's writings are a testimony to the great width of his theological interests. His speculative and philosophical skills are apparent in his works of constructive theology, most notably in his study *On the Trinity*. It was his deep commitment to the unity or catholicity of the Church that energized his ongoing debate with the Donatists, the North African separatists. His polemical ability was brilliantly demonstrated in *The City of God*, his monumental defence of the Christian Church in the face of the attacks of Roman paganism. The matter, however, to which Augustine most fully gave of himself, recognizing it to be the most significant issue facing the church of his day, was the Pelagian controversy, the dispute about the way of salvation. He believed that everything depended on getting this right, on properly recognizing our absolute depend-ence on divine grace in our justification by God.

God's grace, according to Augustine, 'operates' on the human will setting it free from its bondage to sin so that it might choose the good and respond to God in faith; it then 'cooperates' with that will in bringing about a life that loves righteousness. A key text for him was: 'continue to work out your salvation with fear and trembling, for it is God who works in you to will and to act in order to fulfill his good purpose' (Phil. 2.12b, 13).

Pelagius was a lay British monk who was deeply concerned with the widespread growth of moral decadence in the Church. Over the previous decades an increasing number of cultured pagans had found it 'fashionable' to be baptized into the Church, after Christianity had taken on the respectable role of a state supported religion. Pelagius challenged this new generation of converts with the biblical demand for God's people to live holy lives. He was held in high regard both for the purity of his own life and for his consist-ent call to others to practise righteousness. What appears to have triggered his breach with the religious establishment of the day was a passage he came across in Augustine's *Confessions*:

> There can be no hope for me except in your great mercy. Give me the grace to do what you command, and command me to do what you will! (*Confessions*, 10.29, p. 233)

Pelagius believed that such a way of thinking undermined radi-cally the pursuit of personal holiness. He reckoned that if we are only empowered to do what is right by the gift of grace, then those who are morally careless have a watertight excuse for their ongoing disobedience. They do not comply with God's commands for they do not have the natural ability to do so. Surely, argued Pelagius, no one can be condemned for failing to do that which lies beyond their natural capability. Augustine, however, was insistent that although humans no longer have it within themselves to do what was right, yet they are nevertheless required to live righteously. Such righteousness is to be received by them as a gift from God, through his justifying action. If we could be righteous apart from grace then, argued Augustine, salvation would be found in our-selves rather than in God's mercy and Christ would have died for nothing. Believing that this issue lay at the very heart of the gospel,

Augustine gave himself to countering the array of arguments put forward by Pelagius and his followers.

As the discussion developed and the opposing points of view were presented more carefully the differences between the two positions appeared to be narrowing. Pelagius had argued that it was theoretically possible for a person to live without sinning. Augustine initially opposed the idea that humans had the potential to avoid sinning, but came to allow the possibility that the regenerate could in theory act blamelessly (*On Nature and Grace*, 68, p. 145). On the other hand, when confronted by the charge of heresy, Pelagius somewhat surprised his opponents by affirming that we are indeed dependent on divine grace for our righteous actions.

> I anathematize the man who either thinks or says that the grace of God, whereby 'Christ Jesus came into the world to save sinners,' is not necessary not only for every hour and for every moment, but for every act of our lives: and those who endeavour to disannul it deserve eternal punishment. (*On the Grace of Christ*, 1.2)[14]

The antagonists appeared to be saying much the same thing and Pelagius was considered to be quite orthodox by many of those who heard him. Augustine, however, rightly recognized that their positions diverged significantly. Pelagius' understanding of the working of grace was quite different from his own. This is his outline of Pelagius' theory of grace:

> In his system he posits and distinguishes three faculties, by which he says God's commands are fulfilled, – capacity, volition and action: meaning by 'capacity,' that by which a man is able to be righteous; by 'volition,' that by which he wills to be righteous; by 'action,' that by which he actually is righteous. (*On the Grace of Christ*, 1.4, p. 218)

God's grace, according to Pelagius, is given to make us in our own natures capable of righteous action. This is God's work and not our own. We have no say or choice in the natural abilities we have received from God. Our other two faculties – volition and action – are what we ourselves do and in them we are neither directly enabled nor empowered by grace. Pelagius does allow that the law and the prophets can be considered as instruments of grace in that they guide us positively in the choices we make. But both the actual decision to choose the good and the righteous action that follows it, come totally from our own unaided natures. There is in them no direct empowering by the Holy Spirit. Grace gives us the natural capacity for righteousness, but empowers neither our choice to do what is right nor our righteous action. And so it is that although speaking much of grace Pelagius' original position remains unaltered: all humans have it within themselves to obey God's commands. Augustine believes this argument undermines radically the message of the gospel for it encourages us to look to our own inner strength to do what is right rather than to the grace of God and his gift of saving righteousness:

> [I]t is the righteousness of God; that is, the righteousness which we have not from the law, but from God, – not the righteousness, indeed, which by reason of His commanding it, causes us fear through our knowledge of it; but rather the righteousness which by reason of His bestowing it, is held fast and maintained by us through our loving it. (*On the Grace of Christ*, 1.9, p. 220)

This leads us naturally to a consideration of what Augustine meant by 'the righteousness of God', a key notion in any theory of justification.

THE RIGHTEOUSNESS OF GOD

Augustine understands the expression 'the righteousness of God', when used by Paul as a synonym for the gospel (see Rom. 1.17), to refer not to an attribute of God but to that which God brings about in us. It functions grammatically in much the same way as the phrase 'the salvation of God':

> [J]ust as the righteousness of God is used in the sense of our being made righteous by His gift; and the salvation of the Lord, in that we are saved by Him; and the faith of Jesus Christ, because He makes us believers in Him. This is that righteousness of God, which He not only teaches us by the precept of His law, but also bestows upon us by the gift of His Spirit. (*On the Spirit and the Letter*, 56, p. 108)

The righteousness of God is the equivalent of the new righteousness of the believer that God brings about. All that was said of 'the
righteousness of the justified' in a previous section is entailed in
what Augustine means by the righteousness of God. Here the focus
is on its source, there on its result. Such righteousness has a complex relation to the divine law.

THE LAW

Augustine contrasts God's righteousness with the righteousness of
the law, but also outlines the positive relation the one has to the
other.

> This righteousness of God, therefore, lies not in the command-
> ment of the law, which excites fear, but in the aid afforded by the
> grace of Christ, to which alone the fear of the law, as a schoolmas-
> ter usefully conducts us. (*On Nature and Grace*, 1, pp. 121–122)

The law in demanding righteousness causes us to fear, while the
righteousness of God inspires love in us through the Holy Spirit and
brings peace to our hearts. Positively the law, through its threats,
acts as a schoolmaster, by leading us to the grace of Christ. For
Augustine, 'not being under the law' does not mean that we are not
required to fulfil the law's righteous demands, but rather that we
are set free from the fear that it brings to our lives:

> For that man is under the law, who, from fear of the punishment
> which the law threatens, and not from any love for righteousness,
> obliges himself to abstain from the work of sin, without being as
> yet free and removed from the desire of sinning. (*On Nature and
> Grace*, 67, p. 144)

The law is not abrogated as a way of life for the Christian. But the
terror of its threats is removed. The one who is justified has come
to love what the law demands.

CONCLUSION

Augustine's doctrine of justification is a comprehensive theology
of salvation developed within of an understanding of the human

predicament which included the intransigence of human sinfulness, the inability of the will to choose what is right and the dreadful prospect of a final reckoning before God. He argued that on the basis of the sacrificial death of Christ, God graciously liberates our captivated wills so that we might turn from evil and seek his forgiveness. His love is poured into our lives through the Holy Spirit causing us to love righteousness and thereby fulfil the spirit of all his commands. Every good thing we accomplish in our lives is wholly his gift and through this divine generosity the Day of Judgement will be for his people their crowning glory. In Augustine's theology all of these ideas are encapsulated by the concept of justification. It is, in short, divine regeneration and forgiveness working through human repentance and faith. There is no absolute distinction in Augustine's mind between the initial gift of justification received through a loving faith and the reward of eternal life – Gods gracious acknowledgement of the gifts he has bestowed on us. Justification is merited through the gift of a loving faith and eternal life is the final reward for that love in action.

We find here in the writings of Augustine a mature theory of justification in which all its constituent parts are carefully brought into relation with one another in a brilliant synthesis. It is, as one might expect, not a wholly original project, for his thought, like that of all significant theologians, was shaped by the work of his predecessors. What he managed to do, however, was to offer a persuasive, coherent account of the whole subject that dealt seriously with the biblical text and provided a blueprint for the development of soteriology in the Western Church. Most of its ideas have been no more than adaptions to Augustine's original structure.

The question naturally arises, is Augustine's doctrine of justification successful? Does it illuminate our understanding of Paul's meaning? Does it offer a persuasive theological account of the gospel as we find it in the scriptures? In the following chapters we will examine how the Church was led to modify or develop Augustine's doctrine. I draw attention at this early stage in the discussion to two of its apparent weaknesses.

First, although justification in Augustine's thought has to do with the transformation of our lives, he recognizes that at its heart lies an act of divine forgiveness. A much celebrated passage in his response to Julian of Eclanum indicates how important in his understanding of justification is the idea that through it our sins are absolved:

Now, justification in this life is given to us according to these three things: first by the laver of regeneration by which all sins are forgiven; then, by a struggle with the faults from whose guilt we have been absolved; the third, when our prayer is heard, in which we say: 'Forgive us our debts'. (*Against Julian*, 2.8.23)[15]

The notion that a vital aspect of justification is the forgiveness of sin does not fit easily with the idea that justification is merited through a loving faith. This is because forgiveness is not something that is by its nature deserved or merited. An act of pardon functions within a quite different framework from that of reward. It means that the idea that God crowns the gifts he has bestowed on us does not seem to give a proper account of divine forgiveness. In short, it is difficult to understand how justification can be merited by a faith working in love if a central aspect of justification is God's pardoning act. The relation between forgiveness and merit is one which needs further clarification and is one to which the Church was in due course to give much more attention.

Second, for Augustine a faith that operates through love lies at the heart of all the good works that will finally merit eternal life. This, however, also needs to be considered more carefully. Augustine emphasized the Pauline contrast between grace and nature, as well as that between the spirit and the letter of the law in order to secure his position against the Pelagians. But the principal contrast made by Paul to defend the nature of justification is that between faith and works. And it is this distinction that Augustine is unable to employ, for in his thought faith acting in love is the essential form of good works. We need to be alert to the possibility that Augustine's exposition, brilliant though it is, fails to account fully for certain key features of Paul's understanding of justification.

It is with questions such as these in our minds that we turn to consider the theology of the medieval Church and the manner in which it dealt with the Augustinian legacy.

CHAPTER 4

THOMAS AQUINAS

The Middle Ages witnessed a remarkable flowering of theological reflection on the nature and outworking of divine salvation. The concepts of grace, penance, forgiveness and merit were but some of the issues regarding God's redemptive action that were carefully examined in the great monastic orders and considered worthy of public disputation in the newly formed universities of Europe. Although these various schools of theological thought offered somewhat differing perspectives on these matters, they were all profoundly shaped by Augustine's comprehensive doctrine of justification outlined in the previous chapter. By the thirteenth century they had also come under the influence of the writings of Aristotle which had been reintroduced in the West through Islamic mediation. His philosophy was employed by many of the schools as a powerful conceptual tool in their theological reflection and as a resource for refining their increasingly sophisticated forms of argumentation. The study of Aristotle also stimulated a fresh investigation into the relation of faith to reason.

Our particular interest in this chapter is to understand how Augustine's doctrine of justification was modified as it was subjected to close scrutiny and fresh articulation by the schools and theologians of the Middle Ages. Making such an assessment will depend to some extent on which of the often competing schools of thought is considered: whether it be the Dominicans or the Franciscans, the Scotists or the Occamists, the Via Moderna or the Via Antiqua. From the broad spectrum of medieval theology our study in this chapter will focus on the theology of the Dominican Thomas Aquinas (1225–1274) and the manner in which he reworked Augustine's views on justification. His age produced an array of outstanding theologians including Anselm of Canterbury, John Duns Scotus and William of Occam. Thomas, however, has particular significance for Western Christian thought because of the far-reaching influence that his carefully ordered writings have had and continue to have on so large a section of the Church. However, as we consider his ideas we need to remind ourselves that he is but one of a number of conversation partners that we might have chosen for our engagement with the medieval Church.

SCHOLASTICISM

Thomas Aquinas was the quintessential academic. He seems to have been always either learning or teaching. As a young boy he was educated at Monte Cassino by Benedictine monks. Transferring to the University of Naples he encountered a group of Dominicans whose order he determined to join. He went on to the universities of Paris and Cologne where he studied Aristotle under the tutelage of Albertus Magnus. Acknowledged to be a brilliant theologian, Thomas lectured at Paris, Rome and Naples in teaching positions sponsored by the Dominicans. Over the course of his career he wrote on a wide range of philosophical and theological subjects. The most notable among his books were his magisterial *Summa contra Gentiles* and *Summa Theologica*.[1] Although his orthodoxy was not immediately recognized, the Roman Catholic Church was in due course to afford Thomas pre-eminent status among all of its teachers.

The method of education and research in the monastic schools and universities of the period has come to be known as medieval scholasticism. It was a teaching tradition that encouraged the use of logical argumentation and precisely defined terms. Responding to the renewed interest in the writings of the Fathers, particularly those of Augustine, lecturers would provide glosses or comments on their collected texts or sentences. These commentaries would be informed by the principles of logic and philosophy. In a typical lecture a text was read, interpreted at various levels and then meditated on by the students. Finally, questions were raised and discussed as contradictions appeared between the various authorities quoted or other intellectual difficulties surfaced in the text. In the course of time these questions became the most significant aspect of scholastic learning. The complete discussion of a particular question was called a disputation, which could on occasion be a popular public event. In a disputation the arguments against a particular position were first considered, then those in its favour, before a solution was sought. Finally, responses were offered to all of the opposing arguments. The term 'scholasticism' came to be used with negative overtones in much of the later doctrinal discussion. However, the clarity of thought which this method of education encouraged, driven by its commitment to the inherent rationality of theological truth, is surely much to be admired.

Thomas serves as perhaps the most notable exponent of the principles of medieval scholasticism. Let us examine then how, within the framework of scholastic methodology, he reformulates Augustine's doctrine of justification.

THE NATURE OF JUSTIFICATION

To the question 'whether the justification of the ungodly is remission of sins' Thomas answers without equivocation: 'the remission of sins is justification' (*Summa Theologica*, 1.2 q.113 article 1). Equating the two concepts in this way is a remarkably bold theological move. Although Augustine recognized the centrality of the forgiveness of sins in the process of justification, Thomas goes well beyond him by identifying the one with the other. Doing so raises important questions regarding the nature of the righteousness of those who have been justified. If to justify or make righteous means the remission of sin, then being righteousness must somehow be the equivalent of being forgiven. But they appear, certainly in the thought of Augustine, to be quite different notions. One has to do with a God-given set of virtues characterized by love, the other is a state of reconciliation effected by divine mercy.

Thomas responds to this difficulty by offering an analysis of the concept of righteousness. On the one hand, and in line with Aristotelian thought, he holds that righteousness has to do with the right ordering of human action and so righteousness is considered as a personal virtue, whether viewed in relation to one's fellows or to the law. But, according to Thomas, righteousness also denotes a harmony in the ordering of our interior disposition, that is, of our person to God and of the powers of our soul to our reason. Humans were granted this form of righteousness through the original creative act. And so Adam is spoken of in the dogmatic tradition as having an original righteousness. But when this set of ordered relationships was lost through sin and the interior disposition of our being became disorientated or discordant, the renewal of such righteousness could only be established through the remission of sin. For in the forgiveness of our sin, our broken relation with God is re-established or reordered. It is in the sense then of reordered relationships that we are to understand the righteousness of the justified. That is why Thomas is able to argue that justification is simply the remission of sins.

Nevertheless, understanding justification as forgiveness does not, in Thomas' view, mean that we are unaffected subjectively or are personally unresponsive in this gracious act of God. First, he held that in the act of justification there is an infusion of grace in the 'viator' or pilgrim. Forgiveness, as we have seen, implies for him the reordering of relationships, the reconciliation of those who have become estranged. But in order for there to be reconciliation the offender must consciously experience the love of the one offended. Reconciliation is a matter of the heart. The pilgrim requires the working of grace in his or her life to recognize and enjoy the reality of divine love. Without the enlightening action of divine grace there can be no personal knowledge of God's favour and so no effective reconciliation. In short, an infusion of grace is required for the reconciliation of the penitent or the justification of the ungodly (1.2 q.113 article 2).

Secondly, human free-will plays an active role in justification. Thomas holds that God justifies a person in accordance with their nature. He works with us as we are. But it is an aspect of our being to have free-will. So it is that as God moves us to justice or righteousness, he does so by moving our free-will to accept the gift of grace. Some might wonder whether a free-will that is moved by God in this way can really be free. But within an Aristotelian theory of motion, all movement, including that of the human free-will has its ultimate source in the action of the one unmoved mover. The movement of the human free-will can consequently never by viewed as being independent of God's agency. Inhabiting an Aristotelian conceptual world Thomas has no difficulty in affirming the divine moving of our human free-will (1.2 q.113 article 3).

Thirdly, the movement of our free-will in the justifying event is a movement towards God and this initial motion is identified with the exercise of faith. In deference to the authority of Augustine,

Thomas goes on to qualify this movement of faith by allowing that faith is not perfected unless it is quickened by love (1.2 q.113 article 4). Nevertheless, the emphasis in Thomas' thought is that human act of moving towards God is essentially one of believing. Conversely, the movement of human free-will in the justifying event is at the same time a turning away from sin (1.2 q.113 article 5), an act of repentance.

Bringing these thoughts together, it is Thomas' argument that divine justification is an instantaneous but ordered event comprising four elements: 'the first is the infusion of grace; the second, the free-will's movement towards God; the third, the free-will's movement towards sin; the fourth, the remission of sin' (1.2 q.113 article 8). We might say that, for Thomas, justification is an instantaneous event in which, by an act of sheer grace, the sinner is led to turn to God in faith, repent of their sins and receive divine forgiveness. This whole complex, but tightly integrated, process is identified by Thomas with the remission of sins, for that is its proper goal.

It is difficult not to be impressed by the careful logic and illuminating power of Thomas' summary. The complex tapestry of Augustine's doctrine of justification has been reduced to a simple narrative that brings a number of the key concepts into a closely ordered relationship. However, a new question arises when justification is understood in this manner. How does justification interpreted as the initial saving act of divine forgiveness relate to final judgement and the reward of eternal life?

JUSTIFICATION AND GLORIFICATION

In Thomas' thought there is a clear distinction between the justification of the ungodly and the glorification of the just (1.2 q.113 article 9). These two events might be intimately connected in God's saving purpose for the pilgrim, one being the proper end or outcome of the other, but according to Thomas their administration and basis are quite different. Justification is a wholly unmerited gift, while glorification or eternal life is the reward granted to the righteous for what they have done in this life. Further, the determinative human characteristic in justification is faith. The gracious habit which makes an action meritorious is love (1.2 q.113 article 4). This clear distinction between justification and the granting of eternal life is a significant modification of Augustine's thought and the arguments behind it and the implications of it need to be considered carefully.

First, Thomas maintains that justification is a wholly undeserved gift. Augustine had taught that our faith merits justification. Thomas opposed such a view. He understood justification to be the initial instantaneous act of saving grace in a believer's life. As the first act of grace he argued that it could not be merited. Any reward that the pilgrim receives can only be as a form of recompense for what God has graciously done in him or her. As Augustine had taught the Church – God crowns his own gifts. But justifying grace as the first grace cannot be merited. It cannot itself be viewed as a consequence or reward of faith (1.2 q.113 article 5).

Thomas' argument that justification is an unmerited act of grace runs counter to a widely accepted axiom of the medieval Church: *facienti quod in se est Deus non denegat gratiam*. God will not deny grace to the one who does what they can. In his mature writing Thomas came to challenge this notion, recognizing its susceptibility to a Pelagian interpretation, that is, the view that the human response is prior to and so independent of grace in attaining justification (1.2 q.112. article 3). For Thomas, no human act brings about justifying grace.

Second, Thomas affirmed Augustine's view that eternal life is the reward granted to the righteous for their loving actions in this life. The understanding of the final judgement as the just apportioning of rewards is widely attested in the scriptures. 'For we must all appear before the judgement seat of Christ, that everyone may receive what is due them for the things done while in the body, whether good or bad' (2 Cor. 5.10). Now, if the gift of eternal life is merited by the believer, it is difficult to understand how anyone would ever attain it, considering the flawed nature of Christian lives. Thomas is, however, careful to qualify the manner in which a believer merits eternal life from God.

> But where there is no simple right, but only relative, there is no character of merit simply, but only relatively, in so far as the character of justice is found there, since the child merits something from his father and the slave from his lord. (1.2 q.114 article 1)

According to Thomas simple justice occurs only between equals, but there is a relative justice when a father rewards his child or a master his servant. The reward is not required by the strict rules of justice, but it is nevertheless appropriate. It is in this relative manner that God rewards the just with eternal life. It is not a condign merit which justice is required to reward, but a congruous merit, which it is fitting that God should reward but it is not necessary that he does so.

Although eternal life is merited congruously in the sense described above, Thomas believes this does not apply to certain other aspects of the Christian pilgrimage. In both the strict and the relative sense of merit justification is not merited, neither is restoration after serious sin (1.2 q.114 article 7), or final perseverance (1.2 q.114 article 9). Each of these is wholly dependent on divine grace without any regard to human worthiness.

By qualifying the nature and scope of human merit in this manner, Thomas is able to explain the relation of the justification of the ungodly to the final glorification of the just. He does so through his narrative of the Christian pilgrimage. The pilgrim is justified by an unmerited act of grace leading him or her through the exercise of faith and repentance to divine forgiveness and reconciliation with God. Through justification the pilgrim enters a state of grace in which the ministry of the Holy Spirit is experienced. In such a state, grace produces in the pilgrim works of love which merit further grace, an increasingly fruitful process that leads ultimately to the reward of eternal life. Glorification is then the proper goal of justification but is administered on quite different principles.

Within such a scheme of salvation there lies a particular problem. It is a difficulty that was recognized from the earliest days of the Church but is brought into renewed focus by Thomas' narrative. What happens if the pilgrim commits serious sin after having been justified and brought into a state of grace? What happens if the one who has been pardoned falls away from grace, from the Holy Spirit's protecting and empowering action?

MORTAL SIN

In the Gospels, Jesus is recorded as cautioning his hearers that the sin against the Holy Spirit will never be forgiven. It is a warning that has continued to perplex many. There are other similar cautionary passages in the scriptures. The writer to the Hebrews warns his readers that: 'If we deliberately keep on sinning having received the knowledge of the truth, no sacrifice for sins is left but only a fearful expectation of judgement' (Heb. 10.26, 27). So great was the concern about committing them and thereby coming under eternal judgement that some Christians delayed their baptism until their deathbed. In the second century a prophetic figure named Hermas had a revelation that, in view of the near end of the world, one further act of repentance had been granted after baptism.

> [T]hen shall they be forgiven all the sins which in former times they committed, and forgiveness will be granted to all the saints who have sinned even to the present day, if they repent with all their heart, and drive all doubts from their minds. For the Lord has sworn by His glory, in regard to His elect, that if any one of them sin after a certain day which has been fixed, he shall not be saved. For the repentance of the righteous has limits.[2]

This allowance for the possibility of 'once-off' remission of post-baptismal sins was later to be widened. In the third-century Callixtos, the bishop of Rome, announced that all carnal sins could be absolved after proper repentance. Tertullian the first great Latin theologian opposed him strongly, challenging his authority to do so:

> So, too, had the prophets (of old) granted to the repentant the pardon of murder, and therewith of adultery . . . Exhibit therefore even now to me, apostolic sir, prophetic evidences, that I may recognise your divine virtue, and vindicate to yourself the power of remitting such sins![3]

Denial of the faith, however, lay outside such Callixtos' offer of absolution. But even this lone exception soon turned out to be highly problematic for the Church. Apostasy was the main point of issue in the Donatist controversy, the conflict within the Church that arose when many Christians in North Africa opposed the practice of receiving back into the Church the *traditores*, those who had effectively denied the faith by handing over the scriptures to the persecuting authorities. The matter of restoration for those who had fallen away, who had committed an unforgiveable sin, became the cause of a serious division within the Church.

This concern with restoration to a state of grace after the committal of serious sin characterized the life and practice of the medieval Church. And it was in this context that Thomas developed his doctrine of penance. With regard to mortal sins, that is, those sins that lead to death, he held that merit cannot play any part in the pilgrim's restoration. The movement of divine grace leading the pilgrim from justification to eternal life has been interrupted by the offense and the chain of God's gracious actions in the pilgrim's life has been broken. Eternal life is no longer the absolute or condign right of the one who had been justified. Further, the impediment of sin in the pilgrim prevents them from doing acts that have even relative worth or congruous merit (1.2 q.114 article 7). There is, in short, nothing the pilgrim can do to earn their way back to a state of grace.

The urgent pastoral question is 'how can there be restoration to a state of grace after a serious relapse into sin?' The answer, according to Thomas, and in harmony with the then established practice of the Church, is to be found in the act of penance.

PENANCE

Many who have been brought up outside of a Roman Catholic world-view find the doctrine of penance rather strange and have some difficulty approaching Thomas' exposition of it with any openness or sympathy. Some have argued that the medieval Church was confronted with a translation which enjoined the reader to 'do penance' rather than to 'repent'. And it is suggested that this mistranslation of the underlying Greek word *metanoieo* has led Catholic teachers like Thomas to support the extrabiblical practice of penance. I don't think such an argument against the doctrine of penance can be sustained.

Thomas recognizes three elements in the act of penance, that is, contrition, confession and satisfaction (3 q.90 article 3). We might say that for him penance includes sorrow for sin, the confession of wrongdoing, and the mindful determination to put things right. He certainly appears to have an adequate grasp of the meaning of *metanoieo*! In fact, the word penance in Thomas' writing is often no more than a synonym for repentance. When he wishes to distinguish the internal act of repentance from the external sacrament of penance he speaks of penance as a virtue. His doctrine of penance is, in effect, an exposition of the concept of repentance. Let us examine its major features.

At the heart of Thomas' understanding is the perception that there can be no forgiveness of sin apart from an act of inner repentance. He argues that:

[I]t is impossible that God pardon a man for an offense, without his will being changed. Now the offense of mortal sin is due to man's will being turned away from God, through being turned to some mutable good. Consequently, for the pardon of this offense against God, it is necessary for man's will to be so changed as to turn to God and to renounce having turned to something else in the aforesaid manner, together with a purpose of amendment; all of which belongs to the nature of penance as a virtue. (3 q.86 article 2)

We have already seen in Thomas' doctrine of justification that there is a close relation between initial grace, human faith and repentance, and the consequent act of divine forgiveness. There lies in every act of restoration after serious sin a similar connection between grace, repentance and divine restoration.

As to the nature of repentance Thomas distinguishes between penance as a passion, that is, heartfelt sorrow for sin, and penance which is merely an act of justice, that is, the determination of the will to put things right. Further, true repentance is not selective in its operation, it does not focus on one area of wrongdoing and neglect others. 'Consequently a man cannot be truly penitent, if he repents of one sin and not of another. For if one particular sin were displeasing to him, because it is against the love of God above all things (which motive is necessary for true repentance), it follows that he would repent of all' (3 q.86 article 3). Thomas also maintains that inner aspect of repentance is ongoing. 'Because man should always be displeased at having sinned, for if he were to be pleased thereat, he would for this very reason fall into sin and lose the fruit of pardon' (3 q.84 article 8).

Although such an attitude of internal repentance results in divine pardon, Thomas held that it is perfected in the external acts of confession to a priest, absolution by him and satisfaction according to his direction. The scriptural base for such a notion comes from the promises of Jesus to his disciples that take the following form: 'If you forgive the sins of anyone, their sins are forgiven; if you do not forgive them, they are not forgiven' (Jn 20.23). The minister of the

gospel is authorized by Jesus to absolve the penitent by announcing that their sins have been remitted and to guide them in putting
things right, that is, in making satisfaction.

It is Thomas' view that this process of contrition, confession and
satisfaction by the penitent along with the priest's words of absolution constitutes a sacrament of the Church. Why was it so important to establish the sacramental nature of penance? It had to do, at
least in part, with affirming the priority of grace in the divine act
of forgiveness and restoration. The one who has fallen from grace
has no internal resources to merit anything from God either con-
dignly or congruously. The process must begin with God and it is in
the sacraments that Thomas believe his divine, gracious initiative
is held to be found. God might give faith and so justification to the
pilgrim before baptism, even as he will forgive the truly contrite
apart from the sacrament of penance, yet both these acts of remission are perfected in the sacraments.

It was after dealing with these initial questions on penance in
the *Summa Theologica* that Thomas died. The remainder of the
Summa, known as the *Supplement to the Third Part*, was most probably compiled by his colleague Fra Rainaldo da Piperno, largely
using Thomas' commentary on the Fourth Book of the Sentences of
Peter Lombard, written some 20 years earlier. In it there is a careful
outworking of the elements of contrition, confession, satisfaction
and absolution in the sacrament of penance. The dogma relating to
temporal punishment was also considered. Temporal punishment is
the notion that the Church through the actions of the pope, bishops
and priests has been given the keys not only to pronounce absolution to the repentant sinner, that is, the removal of guilt, but also
to prescribe the nature of the punishment that will constitute an
appropriate act of satisfaction. For even when guilt is dealt with
the temporal consequences of sin remain. Satisfaction was understood as the medicine of punishment that heals from past sins and
preserves the pilgrim from future ones. By these penal works the
pilgrim makes restitution for the past and is disciplined for the
future. We see here the link, generally accepted in the Church at
the time, between repentance, restitution and suffering or punishment. Divine forgiveness cancels the guilt of sin but the purifying
temporal punishment remains, for it is the role of suffering to purge
the pilgrim from their attachment to sin. And so, over time, there
had developed the idea of purgatory as a state of suffering after

death where the process of purification could be completed and the pilgrim properly prepared for the eternal enjoyment of God. The Church was empowered through the granting of indulgences to remit all or part of the temporal punishment that it has imposed. It was not initially clear whether it had any authority to remit temporal suffering after death.

The doctrine of penance which was originally intended to clarify how those who had committed a mortal sin might return to a state of grace had developed into a vast and complex sacerdotal system that had become a determinative feature of the spirituality of many Western Christians.

Having offered an outline of Thomas' understanding of salvation, let us take a step back and consider for a moment how different his soteriological structure was from that of Augustine.

MODIFYING AUGUSTINE

A single principle holds together the rich tapestry of themes that make up Augustine's doctrine of justification. God freely inspires a loving faith in the pilgrim and graciously rewards what he has given with pardon and eternal life. The whole process from forgiveness, through growth in a love for righteousness, to the final reward of eternal life is encompassed in Augustine's doctrine of justification and is determined by a single notion. God acknowledges and rewards the love that he instils in us.

Shaped by the theological world-view and methodology of medieval scholasticism, Thomas modifies this Augustinian soteriological structure. Instead of viewing justification as a comprehensive account of the whole process of salvation he makes a clear distinction between the justification of the ungodly and the glorification of the just. There are two quite different, although related principles, operating in these two aspects of God's saving action. Justification which refers only to the initial saving event of forgiveness is an underserved divine initiative in which the determinative human characteristic is faith. Final glorification or the granting of eternal life is the appropriate reward, although not strict desert, for a life that is determined by the gracious habit of love. In short, pardon is freely given through faith, eternal life is the prize granted for a life of loving action.

Making a differentiation in this way between justification and glorification allows Thomas to emphasize the unmerited nature of the former. In the instantaneous but ordered process of initial grace, faith, repentance and forgiveness that comprise justification, there is no indication of merit but only of mercy. The faith that justifies is itself a consequent of initial justifying grace. The consequent righteousness of the justified has to do not with a virtuous way of life, but a new set of relationships, principally reconciliation with God and access into the sphere of his grace. This sphere of grace is a fertile place where gracious, loving habits are formed and flourish as they are rewarded with further grace, leading ultimately to the gift of glory.

The power of Thomas' presentation lies in the clarity it brings to key Pauline themes. Consider how the following summary statement in Paul's letter to the Romans corresponds to Thomas' own account of salvation.

> Therefore, since we have been justified through faith, we have peace with God through our Lord Jesus Christ, through whom we have gained access by faith into the grace in which we stand. And we rejoice in the hope of the glory of God. (Rom. 5.1, 2)

There is a relation in Paul's thought here between present justification and future glory, but as with Thomas it is not direct. Rather, it is mediated through the faithfulness of God to continue the work he has begun by pouring his love into our hearts. Further, Thomas' recognition that final judgement and granting of eternal life has the nature of reward is consistent with the Pauline emphasis and, as we saw in an earlier chapter, with the recorded teachings of Jesus.

Thomas certainly presents a coherent and remarkably persuasive account of salvation. The difficulty, it seems to me, is the manner in which his whole structure is distorted and almost overwhelmed by the attempt to resolve a particular pastoral matter, the problem of mortal sin.

THE PROBLEM WITH PENANCE

Seeking a remedy for mortal sin had characterized much of the spirituality of the Western Church for centuries before Thomas. The manner of dealing with it, namely, the practice of penance, was already deeply ingrained in the Christian mind. Nevertheless, Thomas' own inclusion of the doctrine as an adjunct to his narrative of salvation tended to overshadow and so distort the careful balance outlined above. Let us remind ourselves of that salvation narrative.

The Christian life is viewed by Thomas as a journey from justification to final glorification. Through the initial grace of justification and the exercise of faith and repentance the pilgrim's sins are forgiven and he or she is reconciled with God. A state of grace is entered. In this state, grace produces in the pilgrim works of love which merit further grace, an increasingly fruitful process which leads finally to the reward of eternal life. Mortal sin, however, breaks this saving chain of causally linked events. It places the pilgrim, now spiritually paralysed, outside of the sphere of grace. The predominant concern of those who have committed such sin and understand the implications of their action is their reinstatement. This issue for them is not about their justification – that they understand has been dealt with in baptism. It does not have to do with living in joyful and loving response to the graciousness of God – that is no longer a possibility for they have been excluded from the sphere of such grace. Everything now has to do with being received back into God's favour. It means that repentance and restoration becomes their dominant concern. And it is an anxious affair when repentance is given this central role, for who can be sure that their contrition is heartfelt, that their confession is honest, and that their satisfaction is complete?

The attempt to resolve the issue of mortal sins is, it would seem, an unhelpful byroad for a doctrine of salvation. First, unforgiveable or mortal sins as we find them in New Testament are by definition beyond forgiveness. By engaging in a pastoral process, however, well-intentioned, that details the precise nature of these enigmatic transgressions and then explains how they might be pardoned, takes theology on a path that lies outside the mind-set and practice of the Apostles. There is no suggestion in the New Testament that the pilgrim can repeatedly move back and forth between the kingdom of darkness and that of the God's Son.

Second, in his doctrine of justification as divine forgiveness, Thomas presented a carefully balanced exposition of the instrumental roles of both faith and repentance in gaining pardon. But in the doctrine of penance the requirement of faith appears to be wholly neglected. Instead of looking to the promise of God and the offer of mercy the sinner is encouraged to look inwardly to the reality of their own repentance. But apart from the exercise of faith, these penitential exercises of contrition, confession and satisfaction present an unbalanced view of the Christian response in salvation, one that is bound to focus more on the pilgrim's obligation with regard to sin than it does on trusting in God's gracious promises of mercy. It is a pattern which is bound to encourage human duty, at the cost of trust in divine mercy.

Augustine's understanding of salvation appears to offer a far more stable and secure view of the Christian life, one that delights in God's constancy and mercy, steadfast in the love of God even in the context of our worthlessness and sinfulness. Confession for him is never abstracted from the exercise of a joyful and confident faith. There is in Augustine an assurance of forgiveness not because of the level of contrition or satisfaction but on account of the immeasurable love of God. Grace triumphs over law.

Thirdly, the sacrament of penance as it developed in the Middle Ages and in the theology of Thomas adds weight to the notion that the Church as an institution has been given the keys to life and death and that apart from its priestly ministry there can be no salvation. In this matter, Augustine and Thomas are not far apart. However, the doctrine that the Church through its clergy has the authority to remit punishment is open to abuse. It was the perception that such clerical abuse was being practised on a grand scale that was to ignite the protest movement that challenged first the sale of indulgences and the system of penance and then the whole structure of the medieval understanding of justification. And it is to the articulation of this protest that we now turn.

CHAPTER 5

MARTIN LUTHER

In 1095 Pope Urban II brought an urgent appeal before the Council of Clermont. The Eastern Church had asked for military support in their conflict with the Muslim Turks, who had overrun vast swathes of Byzantine territory and were now threatening Constantinople itself. Urban duly urged the Council members to take up arms in defence of their Christian brothers and sisters in the East. It turned out to be one of history's most significant decisions, giving rise over the following years to a series of bloody crusades against Islamic territories by a coalition of European powers. The consequences of the response to Urban's address still overshadow relationships in the modern world.

One passage in Urban's stirring call for military action against the 'infidel' is theologically significant for the advance it makes on the use of papal indulgences.

All who die by the way, whether by land or by sea, or in battle against the pagans, shall have immediate remission of sins. This I grant them through the power of God with which I am invested.[1]

Some 50 years later Pope Eugene III followed his lead and offered an indulgence to anyone who simply participated in the Second Crusade (1145–1149). Pope Gregory VII went further, issuing complete or plenary indulgences for all past sins to anyone who paid for someone to take their place in the Third Crusade (1189–1192) or contributed in some measure to the enterprise. It would appear that the offer of indulgences for the remission of the punishment of temporal sins had become a standard feature of the Church's fund-raising campaign for military action against the infidel.

Although many in the Church today would oppose such a practice, believing it to be inimical to the teaching of the gospel, it is helpful to follow the logic of the development of the idea of indulgences to understand just how such a way of thinking could have come about. It has always been recognized by Christians that our sins sometimes have temporal consequences and that the earthly suffering we endure as a consequence of our wrongdoing can be spiritually beneficial. Let me offer a contemporary illustration that could happen in any Christian community. It is discovered that a minister has been stealing from his congregation's soup kitchen fund. A judiciary body within the church determines that he be suspended from his pastoral duties for six months; that he work in the soup kitchen during that time and that he pay back all the money that he has embezzled. The penalties imposed on him would in the language of the medieval Church be described as his penance or as the satisfaction that is required of him. Let us assume that after four months there is every indication that the disgraced minister has been genuinely repentant; that he has fully admitted his own culpability in the theft; that he has served the community faithfully in the kitchen and that he has returned all the outstanding moneys. The church's judiciary body now determines that for his own spiritual health and for the well-being of the congregation all the penalties imposed by it on the minister be lifted immediately. In the old terminology, an indulgence is offered.

In the practice of penance the Church originally made a clear distinction between the guilt of sin which is in God's hands and is remitted only through the atoning work of Christ, and the temporal punishment imposed by the Church for the sinner's spiritual purging and discipline. Any temporal sanctions that the Church has put in place can of course be lifted by the Church. Recognizing the value of this purifying process in the sinner's temporal restoration, the question was in due course raised about the need for further purging after death. For it would appear that many die without having been set free from the dominion of sin in their lives. Purgatory, consequently, came to be understood as an after-death state of ongoing but limited affliction, preparing the believer for the eternal presence of God through the cleansing that is brought about through suffering. It was a matter of debate whether the Church had any authority at all over the punishment of those in this state although it was generally accepted that Christians could pray for the relief of those in purgatory. A significant development in the doctrine of indulgences took place in 1230 when Hugh of St-Cher put forward the concept of 'the treasury of the Church'. He argued that it is from the treasury of Christ's merits and those of the saints that the pope is able to draw in order to offer indulgences for temporal punishment. And so the alleviation of temporal suffering became linked with the atonement, that is, the saving work of Christ and the clear distinction noted above between the judgement of God and the penalty imposed by the Church became somewhat confused. The application of Christ's merits along with the merits of his faithful servants for the remittance of temporal punishment was held to be in the gift of the pope.

Some theologians challenged this view of indulgences. Johannes of Wesel, a one-time professor of theology at Erfurt, was brought before the Inquisition in 1479 for declaring indulgences to be a pious fraud. He was condemned to prison for life for this and other views critical of the papacy. The growing concern with the practice of offering indulgences came to a head in Germany in the early sixteenth century during the reign of Pope Leo X. Christened Giovani Medici, Leo was born into Italy's most famous Renaissance family. He was made a cardinal at 13 and become pope in 1513 when he was but 38 years old. He was a profligate spender and within 2 years had exhausted the Vatican coffers. Leo duly appointed 31 new cardinals who were required to advance vast sums in order to take office. One of those in due course to be made cardinal under Leo was Albert of Brandenburg, archbishop of Magdeberg. On acquiring the archbishopric of Mainz he was permitted to have preached in his territory a plenary indulgence for all who contributed to the rebuilding of St Peter's in Rome. The agreement was that he could keep half of the proceeds from the sale of the indulgences to offset his own expenses in acquiring office. It was the preaching of this indulgence by the Dominican Johann Tetzel near Wittenberg that provided the occasion for Martin Luther to enter onto the world's theological and political stage.

THE NINETY-FIVE THESES

Luther was an Augustinian monk teaching theology at the University of Wittenberg. He had been reflecting on indulgences for some time before he went to hear Tetzel preaching nearby. Luther responded to the message of Tetzel by publishing *Ninety-Five Theses* on the power and efficacy of indulgences. Although the form of the theses was scholastic and theologians were invited to debate them, their content was populist and incendiary, not unlike the leaflet a revolutionary might clandestinely distribute.

Luther argued that penance or repentance had more to do with an inner act of deep personal contrition that it did with an external sacramental ritual (*Ninety-Five Theses*, 1, 2).[2] He challenged the notion that the pope had any jurisdiction over the lives of those who had died, on the grounds that only the temporal penalties imposed by the Church could be remitted by the Church (*Ninety-Five Theses*, 8). The value of indulgences, he maintained, was not to be exaggerated for according to him they had nothing to do with eternal salvation. Rather '[a]ny Christian whatsoever, who is truly repentant, enjoys plenary remission from penalty and guilt, and this is given him without letters of indulgence' (*Ninety-Five Thesis*, 36). Luther also indirectly challenged the integrity of the pope in remitting temporal penalties for money, arguing that as Christ's vicar he surely had a pastoral duty to remit them for love (*Ninety-Five Theses*, 82).

For many of his fellow countrymen Luther's theses sharpened the growing perception that, through the sale of indulgences, a form of spiritual abuse was being practised against them by the Church in Rome. A deep hypocrisy appeared to underlie its actions in using the remission of punishment as a tool to raise money for its projects. There were of course a number of complex social, economic and political factors underlying the Protestant Reformation. Significant among these was the influence of humanism, which encouraged an interest in classical texts and their scientific study. But it was the publication and distribution of the *Ninety-Five Theses* that provided the spark for the conflagration which was soon to engulf much of Western Christendom. Although there is nothing of particular originality in Luther's criticism of the practice of indulgences, the public and ecclesial response to his theses propelled him forward on a path of dissent. Disputations with leading Catholic theologians soon forced him to recognize that if he was to defend his *Theses* he would have to allow that both Councils and papacy had erred historically. As Luther came to believe that the Church's magisterium had been quite wrong on indulgences, he was forced to acknowledge that it might be wrong elsewhere and so no longer felt himself bound by its historical decisions and was able to exercise an intellectual freedom untrammelled by an unquestioning allegiance to the dogmatic formulations of medieval scholasticism. Over the following years his ideas on the nature of salvation became the core of a comprehensive theological system formalized in the Augsburg Confession, which served as the confessional basis of the Lutheran Church. And it was Luther's interpretation of justification that lay at the heart of this major project of theological reform. What then was the fresh insight that Luther brought to the doctrine of justification?

DIVINE JUDGEMENT

In an autobiographical fragment of 1545 Luther indicated that his understanding of justification arose out of a new way he came to interpret the key concept 'the righteousness of God' as it is used in the first chapter of Paul's letter to the Romans.

> For in the gospel the righteousness of God is revealed – a righteousness that is by faith from first to last. (Rom. 1.17)

Influenced by his Erfurt teachers it would seem that Luther had at first understood the expression to indicate the attribute of God by which he rewards with grace those who had done what they were able and punishes those who had not. He came to believe, however, that the expression *iustitia dei* referred not to God's rectitude as a judge in the administration of salvation, but to a saving righteousness that he imputes to believing sinners. We will consider this idea more fully below. But first let us deal with a common misconception. A popular interpretation of Luther is that he was a sensitive spiritual man, living in continual fear of divine judgement, who sought unsuccessfully through the scrupulous observance of monastic discipline to find peace with God. His great discovery was that God does not judge humankind but loves us and forgives us freely. This reading of Luther implies that the prospect of divine judgement was simply air-brushed out of his theological world-view as he came to believe that divine condemnation is, in some sense, quite alien to the nature of God. Although such an interpretation is attractive in that it fits closely with a modern religious consciousness it fails to do justice to Luther's thought.

Luther was of course a man seeking to find favour in God's sight, as were countless others who went on pilgrimages, venerated relics, bought indulgences, did penance, fasted, prayed and attended mass day by day. He also shared in a culture in which most people lived their lives with a sense that they were doing so in the awesome presence of God, that is, *coram deo*, never doubting that they were accountable to him for all that they did, said or thought. It was a view that continued to shape and energize his theology. From the earliest days of the Evangelical Movement, Luther argued that seeking to find God's favour by works of the law would result in divine condemnation. God's judgement against even our most worthy actions was to be kept in mind continually by the faithful.

> The law also brings about the wrath of God, – it kills, reviles, makes guilty, judges, condemns all that is not in Christ . . . Presumption cannot be avoided, nor can there be true hope, unless the condemning judgement is feared in every work. (*Theses for Heidelberg Disputation 1517*, 23, 11)[3]

He argued that true repentance leading to salvation begins with an apprehension of divine judgement. ·

> Now, when a man is humbled by the law, and brought to the knowledge of himself, then followeth true repentance (for true repentance beginneth at the fear and judgement of God), and he seeth himself to be so great a sinner that he can find no means how he may be delivered from his sin by his own strength endeavour and works. (*Commentary on Galatians*, pp. 109, 110)[4]

According to Luther, one of the purposes of the law is 'to reveal unto man his sins, his blindness, his misery, his impiety, ignorance, hatred and contempt of God, death, hell, the judgement and deserved wrath of God' (*Galatians*, p. 140). In short, a key aspect of our spiritual blindness, according to him, is our failure to recognize that we are rightly deserving of divine wrath. The law helps us to see things as they really are. In contrast, the role of the gospel is to bring to those who have been humbled by the law the promise of security and peace in the context of divine judgement. The wise pastor knows how and when to apply the law and when to offer the gospel.

It remained then for Luther a paradox impenetrable to human reasoning that the grace of salvation and freedom from the fear of God's condemnation are only discovered where the rightness of divine judgement is properly affirmed. We catch a glimpse of this paradox in his commentary on Jonah:

Notice what a sharp vision the heart must have, to be surrounded by sheer wrath and punishment from God and yet to see and feel, not the punishment and wrath but grace and goodness. That is, to refuse to see and feel them, though feeling and seeing them in the very highest degree, and to see and feel the grace and the goodness, though they are most deeply hidden.[5]

TWO KINDS OF RIGHTEOUSNESS

What is the nature of the righteousness that is acceptable before a holy God? How can such righteousness be attained? Does this righteousness, even in its initiation, lie within human possibilities? These were the great issues regarding salvation that Augustine brought to the theological table. The solutions he offered were by and large received as orthodox by the medieval Church, even though they were modified and developed somewhat by the various movements within it. In the process a new set of questions came to the fore. Can the pilgrim make any preparation for the grace that brings about this saving righteousness? How does he or she cooperate with such grace? How is this state of righteousness to be regained when it is lost through wilful sin?

The issues of salvation, righteousness and grace that had come to dominate theological discussion for a thousand years in the Western Church continued to shape the religious world-view in which Luther found himself. He was, however, dissatisfied with the way the historical Church, particularly scholasticism, had handled them, for in the process it had spawned a host of practices, most notably indulgences, which he believed to be patently at odds with the gospel. And so it was that he returned to the scriptures to try and discover for himself the nature of the righteousness that is acceptable in the sight of God. His key interpretative insight offered a quite new way of reading Paul and thereby of resolving some of the major issues regarding justification which had so engaged the minds of earlier Christian thinkers.

Luther understood the scriptures to teach that in the Christian there are two quite distinct types of righteousness: one passive, the other active. Passive righteousness is so named by him because it is established quite apart from our own contribution. It is an alien righteousness for it comes from outside of us; it is the righteousness of Christ, a righteousness which God imputes to sinners. This passive righteousness Luther contrasted with an active righteousness, a righteousness which we attain in the world of political or civic life; or by the proper observance of ceremony and tradition; or by the fulfilment of moral and divine law through the enabling power of God's grace. It is our righteousness. The clear distinction between these two types of righteousness is, according to him, of critical importance in that it is only through our taking hold of or receiving an alien or passive righteousness and conversely through the renouncement of our own active righteousness that we find peace with God and the forgiveness of sins. Such passive righteousness, Luther argues, lies at the heart of all Christian comfort, providing confidence in God's mercy even as we are beset by temptations and sins.

> This is a righteousness hidden in a mystery, which the world doth not know, yea, Christians themselves do not thoroughly understand it, and can hardly take hold of it in their temptations. Therefore it must be diligently taught and continually practised . . . For there is no comfort of conscience so firm and so sure, as this passive righteousness is. (*Commentary on Galatians*, p. 101)

This perception that the scriptures put forward two clearly distinguishable forms of righteousness generates the principal ideas of Luther's doctrine of justification. Before looking at them more closely, it might be useful to pause for a moment and make a tentative judgement on the validity of using this distinction as a hermeneutic tool in interpreting Paul. To do so consider the following Pauline passages:

> I consider everything a loss because of the surpassing worth of knowing Christ Jesus my Lord, for whose sake I have lost all things, I consider them garbage that I may gain Christ and be found in him, not having a righteousness of my own that comes

from the law, but that which is through faith in Christ – the righteousness that comes from God on the basis of faith. (Phil. 3.8, 9)

That the Gentiles, who did not pursue righteousness, have
obtained it, a righteousness that is by faith, but the people of
Israel, who pursued the law as a way of righteousness, have not
attained their goal . . . Since they did not know the righteousness
of God and sought to establish their own, they did not submit to
God's righteousness. (Rom. 9.30, 31; 10.3)

In these passages Paul makes a contrast between a person's *own*
righteousness and a righteousness that is from God or of God.
Having a righteousness from God is, according to Paul, of ultimate
saving significance. Not only does Luther appear here to be making the same distinction as Paul, but his emphasis on it seems to
bring clarity to texts which other justification theories have generally found to be remarkably opaque. In short, Luther's notion that
there are in the Christian two contrasting forms of righteousness
appears to be a valuable hermeneutical tool in explaining Paul's
concept of justification.

THE RIGHTEOUSNESS OF GOD

The passive, alien righteousness of the Christian is for Luther nothing else than the celebrated 'righteousness of God' in Rom. 1.17.
Such righteousness is for him the essence of the gospel, it is the salvation of God, now fully revealed. Although it was a breakthrough
in his own personal life for Luther to interpret the righteousness of
God not as a divine attribute but as the saving righteousness that
God establishes in the believer, his insight at this point is, in fact, in
harmony with leading strands of the tradition. Luther's conformity
to Augustine is apparent from an earlier quotation we made from
the Church Father's writing:

[J]ust as the righteousness of God is used in the sense of our being
made righteous by His gift; and the salvation of the Lord, in that
we are saved by Him; and the faith of Jesus Christ, because He
makes us believers in Him. This is that righteousness of God,
which He not only teaches us by the precept of His law, but also
bestows upon us by the gift of His Spirit. (*On the Spirit and the
Letter*, 56, p. 108)[6]

Referring to the doctors of the Church, the Catholic theologian
Denifle argued convincingly that 'not a single writer from the time
of Ambrosiaster to the time of Luther understood the passage
(Rom. 1.17) in the sense of the justice of God which punishes, of an
angry God. All, on the contrary, have understood it of the God who
justifies, the justice obtained by faith.'[7]
    The originality and potency of Luther's theological insight is not
that the 'righteousness of God' is that which God establishes in the
believer, for this was already well embedded in the Western tradition, but the distinction he makes between this passive righteousness and the active or personal righteousness of the Christian.

ACTIVE RIGHTEOUSNESS

Luther is aware that his opponents' main charge against his doctrine
of justification is that it encourages a form of lawless. His focus on
an external or alien righteousness seems to suggest that the way
a Christian actually lives does not really matter. To counter such
a perception he is careful to explain the nature of the Christian's
active righteousness. A Christian's own proper righteousness, their
good works, he argues is dependent on the righteousness that comes
from above for its fruitfulness:

> The righteousness of the law is earthly and hath to do with earthly
> things, and by it we do good works. But as the earth bringeth not
> forth fruit except first it be watered from above . . . even so by the
> righteousness of the law, in doing many things we do nothing,
> and in the fulfilling of the law we fulfil it not, except first, without
> any merit or work of ours, we be made righteous by the Christian
> righteousness. (*Commentary on Galatians*, pp. 104, 105)

Our active righteousness is brought about only as we work with
the alien righteousness that is given by God. There are three principal dimensions to this personal or active righteousness of the
Christian. First, it entails a crucifying of the flesh with its passions
and desires. Secondly and positively, it exhibits a love towards one's
neighbour. Thirdly, it is marked by an attitude of meekness and fear
towards God (*Two Kinds of Righteousness*, pp. 88, 89).[8]
    An active Christian righteousness is one that is characterized
not by Christ in his triumph and glory, but rather by Christ in

his suffering. Luther's theology of the cross emphasizes that God is most clearly known through Jesus' freely given sacrificial death and that God's work in us and through us is normally mediated by Christ's suffering. It is in human brokenness and humility that the divine life flows. So it is that Luther emphasized repeatedly that the humble awareness of one's own failures and sinfulness *coram deo* is a central aspect of the believer's active righteousness.

The reader will recognize that there is much about Luther's description of a Christian's active righteousness that is in harmony with, and to some extent dependent upon, Augustine's understanding of the righteousness of the justified. The significant difference is that for Luther this active righteousness, however, appropriate and divinely energized, is not the saving righteousness of Paul's theology. Rather, in the context of receiving salvation it is, he argues, its antithesis.

PASSIVE RIGHTEOUSNESS

Only a passive righteousness, that which is quite alien to the individual, having nothing to do with the way he or she conducts their life and which cannot be contributed to in any way, brings about a person's right standing with God, their righteousness *coram deo.*

It is a righteousness which comes from God and is to be found in Jesus Christ. Luther goes further and makes the bold statement that Jesus is himself our righteousness. Such righteousness is to be contrasted with all human righteousness, which even when divinely energized is no more than filthy rags in God's sight. There is simply no merit, condign or congruous, in our very best actions. And with this radical assessment of human perfidy Luther seeks to undermine the whole doctrine of human merit and all that depends on it. The one who has been truly humbled by the law comes to recognize the flawed nature of their so-called meritorious acts.

> Then he seeth that all the divinity of the schoolmen touching the merit of congruence and worthiness, is nothing else but mere foolishness, and that by this means the whole Papacy falleth. (*Commentary on Galatians*, p. 110)

Rather, Luther argues, God's saving righteousness is freely given in the gift of the Son, quite apart from any worth or merit of our own, or merit which has been wrought in us by God:

> Therefore everything which Christ has is ours, graciously bestowed on us unworthy men out of God's sheer mercy, although we have rather deserved wrath and condemnation and hell also. (*Two Kinds of Righteousness*, p. 87)

Luther understands this justifying righteousness as having two elements. The formal aspect of this righteousness is the exercise of faith in the heart. Where Augustine wrote of faith working through love, Luther speaks of faith alone:

> Faith taketh hold of Christ and hath him present, and holdeth him enclosed, as the ring doth the precious stone. And whosoever shall be found having this confidence in Christ apprehended in the heart, him will God account for righteous. (*Commentary on Galatians*, p. 111)

Faith for Luther is centred on Christ. His favoured metaphor for this justifying faith is of marriage to Christ, whereby all the riches of Christ become ours and all the darkness of our sins is laid upon him. And so it is that in the act of justifying us, that is, making us righteous, God also deals with our sins. He does not impute them to us, but rather imputes to us the righteousness of his son, for Christ has 'wrought works and merits of congruence and worthiness abundantly' (*Commentary on Galatians*, p. 110). Sin remains in the one who has faith and needs to be covered.

> For faith is weak . . . and therefore God's imputation must needs be joined withal: that is to say, that God will not lay to our charge the remnant of sin, that he will not punish it or condemn us for it; but will cover it and freely forgive it, as though it were nothing at all; not for our sake, neither for our worthiness and works, but for Jesus Christ's sake in whom we believe. (*Commentary on Galatians*, p. 130)

Faith in God's provision in Jesus Christ is for Luther all that is required of the sinner. But such faith is not merely mental assent. It is an act that of itself glorifies God even as it takes hold of his Son. There is in it brokenness and humility and a turning away from all of our own resources. It is the only appropriate response we can make in light of the human predicament.

THE HUMAN PLIGHT

As Augustine devoted himself to the task of overthrowing the arguments of Pelagius, that humans have it within themselves to be able to respond to God, so Luther battled with the Pelagian or semi-Pelagian arguments of his own age. Erasmus, the leading humanist of the day, had written a book lampooning the Lutheran understanding of human freedom titled *Diatribe on Free Will*. Luther responded in belligerent fashion with what he reckoned to be one of his most significant theological works, *The Bondage of the Will*. Luther's purpose was to undermine all hope that there is in us a natural ability to choose God. His intention was to make us despair of finding even the smallest grain of confidence in our own capability, including the ability to respond positively to the gospel. Having no confidence in ourselves we learn to seek our salvation only in God.

Where Augustine had argued that we did not have this capacity to choose God because our free-wills had become bound through sin and were in need of liberation, Luther contended that it was our very creatureliness that precluded any genuine freedom of the will. Within the context of divine foreknowledge there could, he argued, be no absolute freedom for the individual. Luther is not suggesting that there is any coercion of our wills. 'The will, whether it be God's or man's, does what it does, good or bad under no compulsion, but just as it wants or pleases, as if totally free' (*Bondage of the Will*, p. 182).[9] Yet all of the actions of the human will nevertheless occur within the determining purpose of God and are constrained by it.

It means that for Luther there is in the human condition not only the presence of radical evil and, therefore, guilt before God, but also there is no possibility of resolving the predicament by our own choosing. There is for us no hope and paradoxically it is in this hopelessness that Luther finds his confidence, in the bondage of his will faith flourishes.

I frankly confess that, for myself, even if it could be, I should not want 'free-will' to be given me, nor anything to be left in my own

hands to endeavour after salvation . . . If I lived and worked to all
eternity, my conscience would never reach comfortable certainty
as to how much it must do to satisfy God . . . But now that God
has taken my salvation out of the control of my own will, and put
it under the control of His, and promised to save me, not according to my working or running, but according to His own grace
and mercy, I have the comfortable certainty that He is faithful.
(*Bondage of the Will*, p. 199)

SIMUL JUSTUS ET PECCATOR

The outworking of Luther's understanding of justification is encapsulated in the statement that the believer is at the same time both
just and yet a sinner. Luther is not here offering the trite observation that there are some serious flaws remaining in the greatest of
saints. Rather, the context in which he used the phrase indicates a
far more radical claim:

> Thus a Christian man is both righteous and a sinner, holy and
> profane, an enemy of God and yet a child of God. These contra-
> ries no sophisters will admit, for they know not the true manner
> of justification. (*Commentary on Galatians*, p. 130)

Luther holds imputation to be the central feature of God's justifying act. Imputation means that an alien righteousness is reckoned
to the account of the godless. They are made children of God and
righteous in his sight, while they are yet sinners. The implication
of this notion for the penitential world of medieval Catholicism
is immense. The vital purpose of the sacrament of penance is to
restore to a state of grace those who had sinned wilfully and so
fallen away from God. The uncontested axiom is that sin excludes
one from grace. Luther indicates that despairing sinners, who are
justified by faith, nevertheless remain in a state of grace. Grace and
sin can coexist!

Luther's doctrine of justification is put forward in a world of spiritual anxiety as a doctrine of pastoral comfort. It offers hope to the
multitudes who despair that God can be gracious to them in the
light of their gross sins. But his words of solace are bound up in
paradox. 'Follow not the judgment of reason, which telleth thee,

that he is angry with sinners; but kill reason and believe in Christ. If thou believe, thou art righteous, because thou givest glory unto God' (*Commentary on Galatians*, p. 131).

CONCLUSION

Luther's complete literary works, which include the notes of his students, form a vast corpus which requires a lifetime of study if it is to be mastered. In this chapter I have tended to focus on the argument from just one significant text, that of his 1531 series of lectures on Galatians. One advantage of this somewhat constricted perspective is that it allows students to examine a very readable book, one that Luther believed to be his best theological work, and weigh up for themselves the thrust of his mature reflection on the nature of justification. It is easy to be so overwhelmed by the mass of learning that one can fail to hear for oneself what Luther had to say. He remains, for those who would read him today, a persuasive religious writer who offers a radical form of spiritual assurance to those who, conscious of their own wrongdoing, live with a measure of spiritual doubt and fear. The Puritan John Bunyan certainly found it to be so:

[O]ne day, a book of Martin Luther; it was his comment on the Galatians, ... had fallen into my hands, the which, when I had but a little way perused, I found my condition, in his experience, so largely and profoundly handled, as if his book had been written out of my heart ... I do prefer this book of Martin Luther upon the Galatians, excepting the Holy Bible, before all the books that ever I have seen, as most fit for a wounded conscience.[10]

I have argued that Luther's key interpretative insight is that in the Christian there are two notionally distinctive types of righteousness – passive and active – and that this insight generated the principle themes of his doctrine of justification. Luther's differentiation between an active and passive righteousness has led to the now widely employed theological distinction between justification and sanctification.

How novel was this insight? Certainly in the development and application of the idea there was great originality in Luther's thought. But a formal distinction between two types of righteousness in the Christian had already been made by Thomas Aquinas some 250 years earlier. Thomas made a clear differentiation between righteousness as the right ordering of one's relationship with God and righteousness as personal virtue. In justifying the sinner, God brings about a right relation with himself which Thomas identifies with the forgiveness of sin. The significance of the distinction between this justifying righteousness and righteousness as a personal virtue of the Christian, Thomas did not go on to explore. I am not suggesting that Luther was dependent on Aquinas for his reading of Paul. It is far more likely that these two very different but equally insightful minds independently recognized the same theme in Paul, that justifying righteousness has to do with forgiveness and is notionally distinct from the righteous life of the Christian.

In developing the idea that there are two sorts of righteousness in the Christian, Luther sought to undermine the rationale behind the whole penitential programme of medieval scholasticism. The following quotation gets to the heart of the matter and clarifies the gulf between a Lutheran spirituality and that of schoolmen like Thomas:

> Therefore the error of the schoolmen is most pernicious, which do distinguish sins according to the fact, and not according to the person. He that believeth hath as great sin as the unbeliever. But to him that believeth, it is forgiven and not imputed; to the unbeliever it is not pardoned but imputed. (*Commentary on Galatians*, p. 152)

According to Luther, those who are justified are righteous before God even when they sin. The Schoolmen held that the actuality of serious sins preclude a person from grace. Now if Luther is right and a justified person remains in a state of grace even when sinning, then the whole rationale for seeking to gain readmittance to God's favour through the penitential system of contrition, confession and satisfaction is undermined. Luther's intention was always pastoral. He was ever seeking to encourage the anxious believer to look not within themselves to their own sinfulness, nor to the divine judgement against such sin, but to the grace of God that had been made known in Christ Jesus.

Did Luther hold that eternal life is finally granted to the believer on the same principles as he or she is originally justified? Although he does not, as far as I know, address this question directly I suspect that the answer for Luther would have to be 'yes'. The logic of his position suggests that on the last day God will reward us according to the alien righteousness of Christ, rather than on the basis of our own, deeply flawed, active righteousness. If this is indeed the case, Luther's position would appear to run counter to the scriptural testimony that the criteria of the final judgement has to do with the deeds we have done in the body – our own active righteousness.

Luther maintained that justification entailed not only the pardon of sins but the active imputation of the righteousness of Christ to the believer. The difficulty with this argument is that although the texts indicate that the believer shares fully in Christ's death and life and all the benefits that arise from it, Paul never speaks directly of the imputation of the righteousness of Christ, rather than the righteousness of God, to the believer. While the theory that Christ's active obedience to the law has atoning significance is one that goes right back to Irenaeus and has a central place in seventeenth-century Reformed dogmatics, it actually has a far more precarious biblical base than is generally conceded.

Finally, there is a deep paradox running throughout Luther's thought. He taught that those who are justified are confident in God's grace but also deeply aware of their own sinfulness before God and of the righteousness of the divine condemnation of their lives. According to Luther the justified person remains a sinner and an enemy of God. And it was this paradoxical aspect of this theology that left him particularly open to attack from his opponents. Those who would defend him felt the need to bring a greater measure of coherence to his thought. Most notable among these was Phillip Melanchthon, who together with other colleagues, gave Luther's ideas systematic shape in the Augsburg Confession, the principal confessional statement of the Lutheran communion. There was another branch of the Protestant Reformation which also paid careful attention to the doctrine of justification, and went on to explore some of the difficulties arising from Luther's exposition. Its intellectual centre was Geneva and its leading figure was John Calvin.

CHAPTER 6

JOHN CALVIN

THE PLACE OF REASON

Luther's doctrine of justification is about divine acceptance in the context of God's righteous judgement. His exposition of it abounds in paradox. He encourages his readers 'not to follow the judgment of reason, which tells you that God is angry with sinners; but kill reason and believe in Christ'.[1] For him a Christian continues to be at the same time both justified and a sinner, a child of God and an enemy of God, *simul justus et peccator*. Faith in God's favour comes to those who are convinced in the rightness of the divine sentence against them. All the threats and warnings of the law are true, but according to Luther they apply to those who are apart from God rather than to his children. In particular, the advice he gave to Christians to 'sin boldly',[2] even when read in its proper context, perplexed many of his followers and was open to caricature by his opponents.

It is not surprising that Luther's detractors sought to criticize the robust presentation of his doctrine for its lack of coherence, for its inherent irrationality. Luther tended, as was his wont, not to defend himself against such a charge, but rather turn it on its head arguing rather that 'reason' was itself the fountain of all human mischief:

> For reason feareth not God, it loveth not God, it trusteth not in God, but proudly contemneth him. It is not moved either with his threatening or his promises. It is not delighted with his words or his works, but it murmureth against him, it is angry with him, judgeth and hateth him: to be short, 'it is an enemy to God' Rom. 8 (:7) not giving him his glory. This persistent beast,

reason I say, being once slain, all outward and gross sins should be nothing. (*Commentary on Galatians*, p. 128)

For Luther 'reason', that is, the reason of the unredeemed mind, lies at the heart of all human sinfulness. Even allowing for a degree of hyperbole in his rhetoric, such an argument suggests a theological methodology that is a world apart from the concern for logic and coherence that had shaped medieval scholasticism. The problem, however, with a theory which does not take seriously the rationality of one's opponents is that it also undermines meaningful dialogue or discourse with them. And dialogue is necessary for persuasion. If Luther's doctrine of justification was to have persuasive influence in the universities, colleges and literary circles of Europe it was required that colleagues like Melanchthon and other Reformers provide a more coherent presentation of it, one which offered a systematic and rational defence of its principal features in the face of the learned polemics of its opponents. Probably the most successful among all those who sought to offer such a justification of these new evangelical doctrines was John Calvin, the young French academic. Within two or three years of leaving the Catholic Church in 1533 he published his *Institutes of the Christian Religion*, a work which in its later and larger editions was to become the most significant theological handbook of the Reformation.

HUMANIST SCHOLAR

Calvin was only 9 years old when in 1517 Luther posted his *Ninety-Five theses* on the Castle Church in Wittenberg. Thirteen years later, when Lutheran theologians drafted the Augsburg Confession, their primary articles of faith, Calvin had barely completed his studies in theology at the Collège de Montaigu, a stronghold of Catholic orthodoxy in Paris. In the years that followed he transferred to Orleans and then Bourges to study law and also immerse himself in humanist learning.

Calvin was by temper an academic, with aristocratic tastes and outlook. His first book was a commentary on a work by the Roman Stoic philosopher, Seneca. He might have chosen to write on this author because Erasmus, the most renowned humanist of the day, had indicated that he was dissatisfied with his own studies on this classical scholar. Through the publication of his commentary

Calvin gained a reputation among the literary elite as a brilliant, if somewhat presumptuous, young humanist scholar.

Soon after finishing this academic treatise, and when he was but 25 years old, Calvin converted to the Reformed faith. History offers tantalizingly few clues as to the reasons behind his decision. He brought with him not so much a set of humanist ideas as a humanist methodology, one which placed high value on the study and scientific appraisal of ancient texts in the original language, along with a voracious appetite for classical literature. His legal studies equipped him with the skills of argumentation and the craftsmanship of a wordsmith, yet without the guile and manipulative instincts that often accompany these abilities. His influence on the shaping of theological terminology in modern French is immense. Calvin certainly had the intellectual tools to construct an ordered defence of the Reformed doctrine of justification in the face of its scholarly detractors. And this was the task faced by those who found themselves in the second wave of Protestant thought. They believed they were called to secure from polemical counter-attack the theological bridgehead gained by those who went before. We turn then to Calvin's exposition of the doctrine of justification. Our principal text is Henry Beveridge's translation of the 1559 edition of his *Institutes of the Christian Religion*.[3]

UNION WITH CHRIST

Calvin held that all the saving benefits and privileges that a Christian receives come only as he or she is united with Christ.

[T]hat so long as we are without Christ and separated from him, nothing which he suffered and did for the salvation of the human race is of the least benefit to us. To communicate to us the blessings which he received from the Father, he must become ours and dwell in us . . . while we on the other hand must be ingrafted into him. (*Institutes*, 3.1.1, p. 463)

This controlling idea of union with Christ determines Calvin's understanding of justification, the nature of the righteousness of God and the place of human merit. The key hermeneutical question for him at every critical point is 'what are the implications for the Christian of being in Christ?' It is within this framework, that is, the believer's union with Christ that he is able to address and define the particular matter of justification.

JUSTIFICATION DEFINED

For Calvin justification is but one aspect of God's saving action towards us. He describes the event in these terms:

> Christ given to us by the kindness of God is apprehended and possessed by faith, by means of which we obtain in particular a twofold benefit: first, being reconciled by the righteousness of Christ, God becomes, instead of a judge, an indulgent Father; and, secondly, being sanctified by his Spirit, we aspire to integrity and purity of life. (*Institutes*, 3.11.1, p. 37)

The essence of the gospel, Calvin argues, is God's gift of his Son to us. Through faith we are united to him and so share in his benefits. Flowing from that union we receive what might be described as 'twofold' grace, that of justification and sanctification. Calvin makes a notional distinction between these two aspects of salvation. The distinction is based on Luther's recognition that there is a difference between the two forms of righteousness found in the Christian: one passive, one active; the alien righteousness of justification and the personal righteousness of sanctification. Much of the Protestant dispute with the Catholic majesterium revolves around this distinction. If justification does not of itself include holiness of life but has to do only with acceptance by God, an event that is notionally distinct from the transformation of life in a Christian, then the Reformed case is well on its way to being established. So it is that Calvin argues forcefully that justification is but one facet of the whole saving event. It is only about our acceptance by God.

> A man is said to be justified in the sight of God when in the judgment of God he is deemed righteous, and is accepted on account of his righteousness; for as iniquity is abominable to God, so neither can the sinner find grace in his sight, so far as he is and so long as he is regarded a sinner . . . He, on the other hand, is justified who is regarded not as a sinner, but as righteous, and as such stands acquitted at the judgment-seat of God, where all sinners are condemned. (*Institutes*, 3.11.2)

The key idea here is that the ungodly person is accepted by God because they are *deemed* righteous. As their lives are sinful they are not in or of themselves righteousness. Having been justified, however, they are no longer regarded as sinners for they have been acquitted at the judgement seat of God. Reduced to its simplest form, this then is Calvin's definition:

> *To justify*, therefore, is nothing else than to acquit from the charge of guilt, as if innocence were proved. (*Institutes*, 3.11.3)

Calvin is able to find support in Augustine for the idea that forgiveness is the central feature of justification, but he acknowledges, as he must, that Augustine viewed justifying grace as that which also transforms the believer's life. Ironically it was Thomas Aquinas who, of the great Catholic theologians, most clearly affirmed that 'the remission of sins is justification' (*Summa* 1.2 q.113 article 1).

In the above precisely formulated definition of justification, Calvin is, of course, dependent on the pioneering work of Luther, but he is also adapting some of the features of his forerunner's exposition. Luther held that justification comprises a formal aspect, that is, the gift of justifying faith and where that faith fails or falls short it is perfected by the imputation of Christ's righteousness. Calvin, however, believed that justification was simply an acquittal from the charge of guilt. For him faith is logically prior to justification, it is not a benefit arising out of it.

THE PLACE AND NATURE OF FAITH

Faith for Calvin is not to be considered as the outcome of justification but rather as the agency through which justification is obtained.

> Here it is proper to remember the relation which we previously established between faith and the Gospel; faith being said to justify because it receives and embraces the righteousness offered in the Gospel. (*Institutes*, 3.11.17)

The potency of the gospel lies in the righteousness secured though Christ. All faith does is receive and take hold of that righteousness as it embraces Christ's person. This relation of faith to justification

is thoughtfully laid out by Calvin in the following carefully balanced outline of the order of salvation:

> The order of justification which it [scripture] sets before us is
> this: first, God of his mere gratuitous goodness is pleased to
> embrace the sinner, in whom he sees nothing that can move him
> to mercy . . . He, therefore, seeks the cause of kindness in him-
> self, that thus he may affect the sinner by a sense of his goodness
> and induce him, in distrust of his own works, to cast himself
> entirely upon his mercy of salvation. This is the meaning of faith
> by which the sinner comes into the possession of salvation, when
> according to the doctrine of the Gospel, he perceives that he is
> reconciled to God; when, by the intercession of Christ, he obtains
> the pardon of his sins, and is justified; and, though renewed by
> the Spirit of God, considers that, instead of leaning on his own
> works, he must look solely to the righteousness which is treas-
> ured up for him in Christ. (*Institutes*, 3.11.16)

Salvation has its source in the goodness of God. It is founded on an
act which originates in God himself – the gift of his Son. Through
such kindness God induces sinners to look away from their own
works and cast themselves wholly on his divine mercy. They are reconciled to God, being justified by the pardon of their sins through
the prayers of Christ. And now renewed by the Spirit they look not
to their own goodness in their daily lives but to a righteousness
wrapped up in Christ.

Any thought that Calvin's logical or systematic skills might overshadow his passion for the gospel or eloquence in proclaiming it
must surely be dispelled by this warm pastoral description of the
role of saving faith. What then, according to him, is the nature of
such faith?

Augustine made a theological proposal of far-reaching significance when he defined 'justifying faith' as a faith that works by
love. He took this to mean that God-inspired loving or charitable
action in the Christian life is itself instrumental in procuring salvation. Calvin, like Luther, generally found Augustine to be an
important ally in the matter of justification. At this point, however, he believed it was necessary to depart from the great African
theologian: 'We, indeed acknowledge with Paul, that the only faith
which justifies is that which works by love (Gal.v.6); but love does

not give it its justifying power' (*Institutes*, 3.11.20). Acceptance with God, according to Calvin, is not brought about by our loving attitudes or actions, but only through our faith.

Further, Calvin understood justifying faith to have stability in its conviction and a certainty in its trust. 'Scripture indicates that the promises of God are not sure, unless they are apprehended with full assurance of conscience; it declares that wherever there is doubt or uncertainty, the promises are made void' (*Institutes*, 3.13.4).

Finally, he argued that the Christian shall embark on no enterprise or service for God apart from faith: 'Nay, here we even insist that no man shall attempt or enter upon any work without faith, that is, unless he previously have a firm conviction that it will please God' (*Institutes*, 3.15.7). Our works are a consequence of our faith.

In each of these arguments, it is apparent that Calvin's exposition of justification is being driven by polemical considerations. This issue at stake has to do with the saving value of good works, that is, divinely inspired deeds of the Christian. For all the protagonists in the debate the matter was ultimately about the attainment of eternal salvation. In his exposition Calvin seeks to lead his readers on a path that encourages them to despair of placing their hope of salvation in anything that had been achieved in or through their own lives, so they might look only to God and his grace for mercy.

A RIGHT ATTITUDE

Understanding the nature of justification is for Calvin a spiritual rather than just an intellectual exercise. It is only in the light of our awareness of the human predicament that the doctrine of justification makes any sense. In particular, it is in the context of divine judgement that we will find the appropriate attitude to deal with its subject-matter.

> In short, the whole discussion of this subject will be insipid and frivolous, unless we sit ourselves before the heavenly Judge, and, anxious for our acquittal, voluntarily humiliate ourselves, confessing our nothingness. (*Institutes*, 3.12.1)

The key issue for Calvin is that we approach God in humility. He believes that as we stand before the awesome holiness of God we will lose confidence in our own worthiness. 'For I call it not humility, so long as we think there is any good remaining in us' (*Institutes*, 3.12.6). He comments on the parable of the publican who enters the temple overwhelmed by an awareness of his own failures. 'Hence we may see how highly our humility is valued by the Lord: our breast cannot receive his mercy until deprived completely of all opinion of its own worth' (*Institutes*, 3.12.7). His argument is that a true spirituality excludes our coming to God with any confidence in our works – in what has been achieved in us.

Like Luther, Calvin understands justification to be an essentially pastoral doctrine. According to him it has a dual purpose. 'Here two ends must be kept specially in view – namely, that the glory of God be maintained unimpaired, and that our consciences, in view of his tribunal, be secured in peaceful rest and calm tranquillity' (*Institutes*, 3.13.1). First, in the gospel we discover that God brings about good among those who do not deserve it. God is glorified in the salvation that he achieves. To claim any merit or just desert in our justification is simply to rob God of his deserved glory.

> If part of the true knowledge of God consists in being oppressed by a consciousness of our own iniquity, and in recognising him as doing good to those who are unworthy of it, why do we attempt to our great injury, to steal from the Lord even one particle of the praise of unmerited kindness? (*Institutes*, 3.13.1)

For Calvin it is a universal principle that whoever glories in himself glories against God.

Secondly, he argues that a doctrine of justification must be robust enough to give confidence to the sinner before the judgement seat of God. There is no value in a doctrine whose promises are undermined by our own manifold weaknesses.

> We gain nothing, therefore, by discoursing of righteousness, unless we hold it to be a righteousness stable enough to support our souls before the tribunal of God . . . To have faith is not to fluctuate, to vary, to be carried up and down, to hesitate, remain in suspense, vacillate, in fine, to despair; it is to possess sure certainty and complete security of mind, to have whereon to rest and fix your foot. (*Institutes*, 3.13.3)

Here lies the essence of the charge he would bring against the Catholic teaching that the good works initiated by God in us merit our salvation. Because of the flawed nature of all human achievement, even divinely inspired achievement, any such doctrine is not able to bring full assurance to the troubled conscience.

It is Calvin's argument that justification is about forgiveness for sinners. According to him such forgiveness is not earned, but freely bestowed. It cannot, therefore, be dependent on what we have done. The problem he faces is that the Bible repeatedly indicates that the outcome of final judgement is directly related to the way we have lived. 'For we must all appear before the judgement seat of Christ, that everyone may receive what is due them for the things done while in the body, whether good or bad' (2 Cor. 5.10). Paul is here reminding his readers of the widely accepted understanding of final judgement, one which appears throughout the New Testament. How then did Calvin explain the scriptural teaching that eternal life is granted to those who have done good deeds?

GOOD WORKS

Faced by the biblical demand for good works, Luther often appeared to sidestep the call to obey the divine law.

> The greatest art of Christians is to be ignorant of the whole of active righteousness and of the law; whereas outside the people of God the greatest wisdom is to know and contemplate the law . . . for if I do not remove the law from my sight and turn my thoughts to grace, as though there were no law and only pure grace, I cannot be blessed.[4]

Calvin, however, sought in a number of ways to take seriously the biblical promises and warnings attached to good works and the obligation on Christians to heed them.

First, he recognized that the law does promise eternal life to those who fulfil its demands. But this, for Calvin, was always only a theoretical possibility. Being who we are, we always fall far short of the just requirements of the law. Our good works are simply not good enough. 'We, indeed, hold with Paul, that those who fulfil the Law are justified by God; but because we are all far from observing the Law, we infer that the works which should be most effectual to

justification are of no avail to us because we are destitute of them'
(*Institutes*, 3.11.15, p. 52). Calvin looks to the authority of Augustine
to support his case:

> Still the observation of Augustine is true, that all who are stran-
> gers to the true God, however excellent they may be deemed on
> account of the virtues, are more deserving of punishment than
> of reward, because, by the pollution of their heart, they con-
> taminate the pure gifts of God [August. Contra Julian. Lib. iv.].
> (*Institutes*, 3.14.3)

Second, he argues that only the works of the person who has
already been reconciled to God can find favour with him. Again
he finds support in Augustine: 'For this reason, Augustine says,
"Our religion distinguishes the righteous from the wicked, by the
law, not of works but of faith, without which works which seem
good are converted into sins" [August. ad Bonif. Lib. iii. c.v]'
(*Institutes*, 3.14.4).

It is important to note, however, that Calvin is not here conceding
that the divinely inspired good deeds of Christians are themselves
meritorious of salvation. Even that which God has done through
us, he argued, is flawed and that on two counts:

> That no believer ever performed one work which, if tested by
> the strict judgment of God, could escape condemnation; and,
> moreover, that were this granted to be possible (though it is not),
> yet the act being vitiated and polluted by the sins of which it is
> certain that the author of it is guilty, it is derived of its merit.
> (*Institutes*, 3.14.11)

Third, Calvin does allow that the believer may be bolstered in their
faith by their works, interpreted as the marks of divine favour in
their lives.

> Wherefore, when we exclude confidence in works, we merely
> mean, that the Christian mind must not turn back to the merit of
> works as an aid to salvation, but must dwell entirely on the free
> promise of justification. But we forbid no believer to confirm
> and support this faith by the signs of the divine favour towards
> him. (*Institutes*, 3.14.18)

Fourth, Calvin argues that although works are not themselves the ground of salvation they are nevertheless a necessary element in the redemptive process.

> For this reason, he [Paul] sometimes makes eternal life a consequent of works; not because it is to be ascribed to them, but because those whom he has elected he justifies, that he may at length glorify (Rom viii.30); he makes the prior grace to be a kind of cause, because it is a kind of step to that which follows. (*Institutes*, 3.14.21)

This is a key element in his argument. Good works are necessary for salvation, but are not in themselves meritorious. Because justification and sanctification are inseparable, everyone justified will be made holy and do good deeds. Both of them flow from our union with Christ and logically imply one another. Eternal life is given to those who do good deeds, but the ground for their acceptance with God is the righteousness that is found in Christ, not the deeds which they have done.

Fifth, although Calvin finds the medieval concept of merit extremely misleading when applied to human action he acknowledges that God does find pleasure in our works. His explanation of how this happens is not so different from the scholastic theory of congruent value.

> First, God turning his eye away from the works of his servants which merit reproach more than praise, embraces them in Christ, and by the intervention of faith alone reconciles them to himself without the aid of works. Secondly, the works not being estimated by their own worth, he, by his fatherly kindness and indulgence, honours so far as to give them some degree of value. Thirdly, he extends his pardon to them, not imputing the imperfection by which they are all polluted, and would deserve to be regarded as vices rather than virtues. (*Institutes*, 3.17.3)

We see then that Calvin repeatedly affirms the value and place of good works in the Christian life. What he will not allow, however, is the idea that these works may serve as some sort of effectual cause to bring about the forgiveness of sins. They are not, he argues, in any way instrumental in our justification.

In the above discussion Calvin's doctrine of justification had been presented as a reworking of Luther's ideas of the subject. I have suggested that the *Institutes* provide a carefully constructed and reasoned defence of the central ideas regarding salvation which had been so vigorously championed by the German Reformer. Of course, there is some reshaping of his doctrine in the process, but one is able to discern in all Calvin's writing a deep and abiding respect for the pioneering initiative of his forerunner.

If the theology of Luther has shaped Calvin's exposition so too have the arguments of his leading Catholic opponents. As we have indicated polemical concerns underlie almost every aspect of his presentation. What were these concerns? And more specifically what were the principal points of difference between Calvin and the Catholic Church?

A CATHOLIC PERSPECTIVE

So divisive was the debate over justification between the Reformers and the Catholics that the subtlety of the theological differences between their positions was often lost when it was presented to later generations. It is generally far easier in a polarized discussion to parody the arguments of one side or the other rather than to try and understand the subtlety of the issues at stake.

There was, as we have seen, considerable development in the Reformed understanding of justification in the decades following Luther's initial challenge to the Roman Church. Likewise there was a great deal of fresh theological thought given to the subject of justification by leading Catholic theologians as they responded to the Protestant doctrine. The official summary of Catholic teaching on the matter is to found in the Council of Trent's decrees on justification arising from its sixth session sitting in 1547. Here is my synopsis of that text.

Fallen humans are all subject to divine condemnation and together lie under the power of evil. They are unable by their own free-will to liberate themselves from the bondage in which they find themselves. God, however, has given his Son so that through faith in his blood their sins might be propitiated. Only by being born again in Christ do the unrighteous receive the grace that will justify them, making them to be righteous and thereby delivering them from the kingdom of darkness. This event of justification is initiated by God himself, quite apart from any human merit. Through his predisposing grace sinners are called of God and enabled to respond to and cooperate with grace in the process of their justification. Aided by such grace they come to believe that God's people are graciously justified by God through the redemption that is in Jesus and, in particular, they come to trust that God will be propitious to their own persons for Christ's sake. Learning to love God they turn from sin which they begin to detest and begin a new life of obedience to God. Justification is then not only the forgiveness of sins but the sanctification and renewal of the inner person through the voluntary reception of the grace and gifts which turn a person from being unrighteousness to being righteousness. Unless these gifts of faith, hope and love are infused into a person's life he or she is neither united perfectly with Christ nor made a member of his body. Justification is said to be through faith because faith is the foundational act of human salvation. It is said to be gracious or freely given because none of those things which precede justification whether faith or works are able to merit justifying grace. Finally, through obedience to the commands of God, faith combines with good works to bring about a continual increase in justification or righteousness.

Many Protestants on reading this summary of the official Catholic understanding of justification will be surprised that there is so much of it with which they would agree. Unfamiliar expressions such as 'predisposing grace' don't immediately suggest major error and the differences that certain phrases in the text have with classical Reformed statements appear to be peripheral. What then are the key points of difference between Calvin and the doctors of theology meeting at Trent, between Geneva and Rome in the matter of justification?

First, Trent does not believe that a nominal distinction between justification and sanctification can or should be made. It does not concede Luther's central thesis that there is in scripture a clear distinction made between an active or personal righteousness and a passive or external righteousness, which can be called the righteousness of God. Although there appears to be a convergence of language about justification in the formulations, the view, fundamental to the Reformed faith, that justification has to do with the imputation of an alien righteousness is not accepted. Put in another way Trent does not concede that justification is equivalent to the forgiveness of sin.

Second and flowing from the first difference, Trent holds that justification is an ongoing process that is continuous and developing and so incomplete in this life. There can, therefore, be no firm assurance for the believer that he or she has been accepted of God: 'even so each one, when he regards himself, and his own weakness and indisposition, may have fear and apprehension touching his own grace; seeing that no one can know with a certainty of faith, which cannot be subject to error, that he has obtained the grace of God' (chapter IX). The widespread existence of such spiritual uncertainty in the face of final judgement helps to explain why Luther, and Calvin after him, sought so strenuously to present justification as a pastoral doctrine, one which was able to provide assurance to troubled consciences. For them justification was a complete and perfected act of God that gave full assurance of peace. 'Therefore, since we have been justified by faith we have peace with God' (Rom. 5.1).

Third, Trent was far more optimistic about the ability of humans to act righteously than either Luther or Calvin. It argued that a justified person was able to fulfil the divine commands:

> [N]o one ought to make use of that rash saying, one prohibited by the Fathers under an anathema, – that the observance of the commandments of God is impossible for one that is justified. For God commands not impossibilities, but, by commanding, both admonishes thee to do what thou are able, and to pray for what thou art not able (to do), and aids thee that thou mayest be able. (chapter XI).

Calvin, as we have seen above, denied that Christians, even when empowered by the Spirit, were able to fully satisfy the holy demands of God. It is interesting that it was Pelagius who had argued against Augustine that God does not demand of us what we cannot achieve.

Luther and Calvin's purpose in denying humans the ability to ever fully satisfy God's law was to encourage them to cast themselves wholly on God's strength and mercy. The Catholics believed that the denial of human ability to please God would lead to despair and moral apathy.

Fourth, Trent believed that good works in a Christian did merit further grace and so increase justification. Calvin strong opposed this. It is interesting, however, that in the matter of works Calvin is in many ways remarkably close to the Catholic position. He would not allow that good works merited justification, but he would have granted that fervent Spirit-inspired prayer, for instance, might bring about a growth in spirituality. The problem is that the opposing sides meant quite different things by justification. Further, Calvin conceded that eternal life is a reward given for the way justified people have lived. His argument, however, was that salvation was not merited by good works. They were simply a necessary step between justification and glorification in the order of salvation. That which merited salvation was the righteousness of Christ which was to be apprehended only by faith.

CONCLUSION

Luther had argued for the justification of the ungodly by faith alone. By embracing in Christ an alien righteousness, a righteousness that comes from God, sinners could take comfort that they were now reconciled with him. Luther's presentation was rough, robust and rhetorical and was received by the common people of Germany and beyond with great joy.

Calvin's task was to take this doctrine, which had now come under widespread intellectual attack, and by reworking its arguments persuade a reflective jury of his humanist peers that it was indeed the appropriate way to read these ancient Pauline texts.

He argued that every spiritual blessing and benefit that believers are promised is to be had only in so far that they are united to Christ. For those who are indeed in Christ there is a twofold aspect to the divine grace that is received – justification and sanctification. Justification is simply the forgiveness of sins. As they are united with Christ, his righteousness is properly reckoned to be theirs. They are then a people without guilt. Those who would understand and receive these things must approach God in humility. Standing in awe before the throne of the all-seeing God they will learn not to look to any qualification in themselves, any deeds they have accomplished, as grounds to merit his mercy. They will find confidence only in what Christ has accomplished on their behalf. Those whom God justifies he will also sanctify by his Spirit, making them to be holy. Although eternal life is promised to them as a reward for what God has done in them, it is merited only through the life and death of Christ.

Calvin's debate with Catholicism over justification was but one aspect of the collision of Renaissance humanism with the Catholic tradition; of the competing authority of the classical texts, in this case the Bible, with the authority of the Church as it is embodied the teaching of its councils and doctors. The emergence of a Protestant understanding of justification cannot be explained adequately apart from the Renaissance, the flourishing of learning during this period emerging from the study of classical documents. It created a mind-set which enabled Christians to challenge the traditions of their Church in the light of their study of the ancient sources.

In the decades which followed the publication of the *Institutes* a swathe of reflective Christians in Western Europe found themselves persuaded by Calvin's arguments. It was not too long, however, before the scientific revolution and the epistemological questions that were to shape the Enlightenment gave birth to a new set of challenges to the Christian faith and its doctrine of justification.

CHAPTER 7

FRIEDRICH SCHLEIERMACHER

THE CHALLENGE OF A CHANGING WORLD-VIEW

The Renaissance was a significant cultural movement that is generally held to have originated in fourteenth-century Florence before spreading to the other major cities of Europe. It was considered to be a 'rebirth' of sorts for it placed particular value on the achievements in architecture, art, philosophy and literature of ancient Rome and Greece. The revitalized interest in the writings of classical authors stimulated learning and gave rise to the development of linguistic and hermeneutic skills which were necessary for the study of these ancient texts. This enthusiasm for classical culture in all its forms tended, however, to overshadow the significance and respect given to some of the major intellectual achievements of the medieval period.

In matters of religion there was, as might be expected a certain tension between the place that Renaissance scholars afforded the ancient biblical texts and the Catholic Church's long-standing loyalty to the whole dogmatic tradition of the Church, particularly, the more recent scholastic developments of the late Middle Ages. The debate, outlined in the previous two chapters, between Protestants and Catholics over the meaning of justification can be viewed, at least in part, as an outworking of the collision of these competing loyalties. Time and again a choice had to be made between the authority of the scriptures over against that of the whole theological tradition. The impetus that Renaissance humanism gave to the Protestant Reformation in this instance is a reminder that a changing world-view brings with it new challenges to Christian thought and practice and sometimes requires that its formulations be defended afresh or presented in quite new ways. Of course, new world-views themselves also stand in need of constant critique.

After the Renaissance a transformation in the way we understand the material world brought even more significant intellectual challenges to the faith and doctrine of the Church. The seventeenth and eighteen centuries witnessed a change of intellectual outlook in Europe so radical that commentators have described it simply as the Enlightenment. It was as though those caught up in it had been led out of darkness into the light. What brought about this new confidence in understanding and interpreting the world? It was, in a nutshell, the emergence of modern science. In the mid-sixteenth century Nicolaus Copernicus had presented a reasoned argument for his theory that the earth and other planets orbited the sun, and that the earth was consequently not the physical centre of the universe. His arguments became the most celebrated example of a completely new way of discovering truth. His heliocentric theory was in due course supported by Galileo's astronomical observations and Kepler's laws of planetary motion, thereby in a comparatively short space of time totally undermining the generally accepted cosmology of Aristotle and the official church teaching on the matter. The lesson was clear, truth in such matters was to be discovered not from the careful reading of ancient texts, nor from the pronouncements of the theologians of the Church, whether Catholics or Protestants, but through careful observation and reasoned deduction. And so the question came to be raised in almost every area of human intellectual endeavour – how do we know what we know? How can we be sure of what we hold to be true? How is truth to be found? Epistemology became the dominant philosophical issue of the age.

Questions regarding the basis of our knowledge were soon applied to the Church's theological dogma. On what grounds do Christians believe what they do? In the face of such challenges it became increasingly important for the Church to offer some sort of explanation for the epistemological foundations of its central doctrines. Theologians such as Anselm and Aquinas had long since reflected on the relation of faith and knowledge, of theology and science. But the spectacular recent advances of science in the fields of natural physics, chemistry and medicine along with the development of mathematics suggested to many in the late seventeenth century that the relation of theology and science was not one of two equal partners but more like that which exists between superstition and fact.

One of the strategies of the Church in the face of these intellectual challenges was to appeal to the occurrence of miracles as a way of providing empirical validation for the truth of its central doctrines such as the divinity of Christ. The recourse to miracles, however, as an epistemic foundation for faith was always going to be a circular way of reasoning, for faith is clearly required to believe in a miracle, particularly, for those who had not been present to witness it. Further, when the study of history began to be treated as a science, one of its fundamental principles was that historical events must be interpreted in the light of their correspondence to similar happenings. Miracles, being 'out-of-the-ordinary' occurrences, were consequently by their very nature discounted by 'objective' historians. As this new historical method came to be applied to the person of Jesus, his life-story was retold, stripped of all the miraculous embellishments of faith with which the Church was held to have clothed him. These new perspectives meant that in many literary circles the dogma of the Church became intellectually discredited and was often seen as no more than a tool used by the clergy to inhibit the enlightenment of lay minds. Many remembered that Copernicus had been declared a heretic by the Church and Galileo, who supported his heliocentric model, was tried by the Inquisition and forced to recant.

How was one persuasively to present afresh the historic faith of the Church in such an intellectual climate? Friedrich Schleiermacher (1768–1834), generally considered to be the father of modern theology, made an heroic attempt to do precisely this.

DOCTRINE AS THE STUDY OF HUMAN SPIRITUALITY

The new scientific approach developed in the sixteenth and seventeenth centuries was known as the empirical method. Empiricism is the view that knowledge is to be gained by examination and experimentation rather than by intuition, a priori reasoning or revelation. Empiricists were of course quick to recognize that the observer does not have direct experience of the world. His or her knowledge is, they held, always mediated through the senses. And so the view emerged that 'certain' knowledge could only be obtained of that which was theoretically open to experience by our senses. Within such an intellectual perspective it was clearly difficult to explain how one could have any 'sure' knowledge of an immaterial god?

The philosopher Immanuel Kant sought to find a place for our knowledge of God within this new epistemological framework. He argued that other than the knowledge that is derived from our experience of the phenomena of the world there is a practical knowledge that pertains to matters such as ethics. He maintained, for instance, that there are good reasons for an individual to be persuaded that certain ways of behaving are 'categorically imperative'. In close relation to this world of practical ethics Kant located religious knowledge. He argued that without the postulation of God's existence and a doctrine of final judgement ethical cohesion would collapse. And so it was that fields such as ethics, religion and aesthetics found themselves holding a secondary or derived status within this newly constructed hierarchy of knowledge.

Schleiermacher sought a more secure epistemological foundation for Christian doctrine, one which would be better protected from the damaging attacks of philosophers, scientists and historians. He took the highly imaginative step of proposing that the proper subject of theology is not God as he is in himself, nor God as he is known through his action in the world, a realm that is open to our sense experience. Rather, he argued, the appropriate subject-matter of theology is human spirituality or piety. And the essence of human spirituality, according to Schleiermacher, is not about what we believe or how we act, but about how we feel. It has to do, in the language of his time, with our affections. His revolutionary proposal was that: 'Christian doctrines are accounts of the Christian religious affections set forth in speech' (*The Christian Faith*, 15, p. 76).[1] In his rather technical style he explains what these affections are:

> The common element in all howsoever diverse expressions of piety, by which these are conjointly distinguished from all other feelings, or, in other words, the self-identical essence of piety, is this: the consciousness of being absolutely dependent, or, which is the same thing, of being in relation with God. (4, p. 12)

In short, all theology is no more than a careful and systematic analysis of our conscious feeling of absolute dependence on God.

The proposal that all Christian doctrines are no more than accounts of Christian religious feelings set forth in speech is not to suggest that doctrines are the compilation of empirical data collected from a range of Christian believers who have shared with a team of researchers the nature of their religious experiences. Not at all. The process was a wholly rational one that took place in Schleiermacher's study and flows out of his understanding of religious affections. His intention was to construct a body of Christian doctrine, outwardly similar to that which is found in classical Protestant dogmatics, that is based on the implications of this particular aspect of human spirituality – the consciousness we have of being absolutely dependent on God.

The reader unacquainted with the work of Schleiermacher will find it difficult to conceive how, from the analysis of this one aspect of Christian self-consciousness, it could be possible to generate a whole systematic theology which had an influence on succeeding generations equal to that of Calvin's *Institutes.* But that is precisely what Schleiermacher achieved with his opus magnus *The Christian Faith.* It brought about a radical shift in the primary focus of religious thought from the being of God and his creative and redemptive actions in history to that of the human subject and his or her experience of divine salvation. In it one can detect the influence of Schleiermacher's early Pietism with its stress on the value of personal religious experience rather than dogma about God or the details of sacred history. The revolution that *The Christian Faith* brought about was shaped by a dramatic shift from objectivism to subjectivism in theological approach.

Our particular interest in this study is to examine how this change of approach led to a quite new way of understanding both the human predicament and divine justification. Let us consider some of the ideas that resulted from this new way of doing theology.

FAITH IN GOD

Does Schleiermacher imply that the proper subject-matter of theology is human religious experience rather than God? It certainly appears so. But an argument can be made that in his thought our consciousness of being absolutely dependent on God does have a proper reference to a much greater being or entity existing outside of ourselves. It is apparent, however, that Schleiermacher did not hold that our consciousness has any clear innate conceptual understanding of such a being. All that we are conscious of is that there is an object outside of ourselves on which we are wholly dependent. We also need to remember that for Schleiermacher our religious consciousness is primarily a self-consciousness. This means that the fact that we have a certain religious feeling indicates something about us but does not guarantee the truth of our interpretation of that feeling.[2]

What in such a context does it mean to have faith? Schleiermacher refers to an earlier discussion:

> [W]e spoke about faith in God which was nothing but the certainty concerning the feeling of absolute dependence, as such, i.e. as conditioned by a Being placed outside of us, and as expressing our relation to that Being. (14.1, p. 68)

Faith is a certainty about our feelings and our feelings are a fact of our experience. Whether such feelings correspond accurately with an external reality does not appear to be an issue. All that is required according to Schleiermacher is that there is such an object on which we feel dependent.[3] Faith in God is being sure that we are indeed wholly dependent on that external reality.

SIN

Schleiermacher's understanding of sin is derived from his analysis of the human consciousness of being dependent on God. He holds that:

> We have the consciousness of sin whenever the God-consciousness which forms part of an inner state, or is in some way added to it, determines our self-consciousness as pain; and therefore we conceive of sin as a positive antagonism of the flesh against the spirit. (66, p. 271)

This sense of pain which sin brings about is closely related to a feeling of separation from God:

> [T]he distinctive feature of Christian piety lies in the fact that whatever alienation from God there is in the phases of our experience, we are conscious of it as an action originating in ourselves, which we call Sin. (63, p. 262)

It is important to recognize that in Schleiermacher's exposition sin is not to be objectified as though sin is some sort of reality existing outside of our mind. 'On the contrary, we must rather insist upon the fact that sin in general exists only in so far as there is a consciousness of it' (p. 277). Sin is not then defined in terms of a breach of divine or natural law or as the evil that we might bring upon our fellows. It has to do with our consciousness of pain and separation from God which we perceive as flowing from our actions. It is a subjective or internal matter rather than an external objective reality. From the human side sin is experienced as a sense of pain and a consciousness of estrangement from God. But how is sin conceived from God's side?

THE JUSTICE OF GOD

When Schleiermacher attributes certain characteristics to God such as justice he is quite clear that he is merely proposing qualities of God or ways of behaving that arise from an analysis of human piety. The proper subject-matter of theology, as he conceives it, allows him to go no further than this. What, according to Schleiermacher, can be said of the justice of God from an examination of our religious affections?

> The justice of God is that divine causality through which in the state of universal sinfulness there is ordained a connexion between evil and actual sin. (84, p. 345)

We are conscious of a relation between sin and evil or misfortune. The concept of God's justice is what we posit as the effective cause of that connection. In short, it is the justice of God that brings about appropriate suffering for sinful action. Schleiermacher defends his decision to define divine justice in this rather narrow way. He argues that this justice must be retributive, that is, it has to do with the giving of rewards and punishment rather than issues of governance and fair distribution which he believes are more appropriately referred to the divine wisdom. Further, the idea of reward is something that Christian piety always consigns to grace and the person of Christ rather than to its own action. Divine justice then, according to Schleiermacher, has to do only with the punishment of sin.

Now the fixed relation of punishment to sin is true only in corporate life which is a unity complete in itself. In the case of individuals we do not see that relationship existing. Civil justice with respect to individuals is often grossly unfair and many sinful actions remain unpunished. There is no clear correlation in this life between the sin of an individual and his or her suffering. To hold that future judgement will resolve this issue is simply to put the difficulty further away for we have no experiential insight into the relation between sin and suffering in a future state. According to Schleiermacher, it is the justice of God that establishes the relation between sin and punishment in corporate life.

What is the purpose or value of this divine punishment of sin? First, these penalties cannot be reformative otherwise there would be no need for grace. Schleiermacher argues that: 'It is also obvious that if the God-consciousness could be strengthened by punishment, as system of punishment as perfect as possible could have been made to serve instead of redemption' (84.3, p. 350).

Second, the purpose of divine punishment could not be vengeance or mere retribution. For such retribution 'is inflicted only in so far as the injured person regards his pleasure in the suffering of the injurer as removing or assuaging his own pain (84.3, p. 350). Such vengeance or retribution is, he believes, unworthy of God. According to Schleiermacher:

> Divine penalties of such a type, however, could be believed in only at a very primitive stage of development – a stage at which the Deity is still thought of as susceptible to irritation, and as not above feeling an injury or having other passive states. (84.3, p. 350)

Third, the only purpose of the punishment of sin in the communal life is that it might serve as a deterrent to wrongdoing. It is to prevent the unchecked sensuous tendencies of the sinner gaining mastery over his or her life. It is only relative to the coming of redemption that this restraining role of divine justice can be properly understood. And so it is the argument of Schleiermacher that the justice of God is that which holds sin in check before the coming of redemption, a role that theologians before him had generally ascribed to the law.

Such a view profoundly affects the Christian understanding of the human plight. From the earliest times the Western Church considered the prospect of divine judgement on account of sin to be the most serious predicament facing humankind. But such a view can have no part in Schleiermacher's system. Any suffering in the community as a consequence of sin can serve only as a restraint until the time of salvation. There is no sense in which God is offended by our wrong-doing. Once we leave behind primitive anthropomorphic notions of God we recognize that nobody can ever be the object of his anger:

> This does not in the least mean that previously (man) was the object of divine displeasure and wrath, for there is no such object. (109.4, p. 503)

The corollary of such a view in Schleiermacher's thought is that there can be no place for divine mercy. For mercy has to do with an act of pardoning grace to those deserving of punishment, to those who live under God's displeasure and Schleiermacher does not believe that anyone falls into this category. The concept of mercy should not then be applied to God in a dogmatic or literal sense:

> To attribute mercy to God is more appropriate to the language of preaching and poetry than to that of dogmatic theology. (85, p. 353)

If divine salvation is not about the expression of mercy in the face of divine judgement, what is it in Schleiermacher's interpretation of redemption?

THE PERSON AND WORK OF CHRIST

Faithful to his theological method Schleiermacher expounds the particular dignity of the person of Jesus in concepts that are derived from his analysis of human piety.

> The Redeemer, then, is like all men in virtue of the identity of human nature, but distinguished from them all by the constant potency of His God-consciousness, which was a veritable existence of God in Him. (94, p. 385)

It is in terms of this potency of Jesus' God-consciousness that Schleiermacher describes his high status: 'for to ascribe to Christ an absolutely powerful God-consciousness, and to attribute to Him an existence of God in Him, are exactly the same thing' (94.2, pp. 386, 387).

Whether this status is, in fact, that of a divine being is not immediately clear. God-consciousness or being in a relation with God is a state that all the redeemed come to experience. If this is all that determines Jesus' high standing, it would seem that his difference from other pious men and women is merely one of degree. If this is so, Jesus would be no more that the ideal of human piety. This is a way of conceiving him that Schleiermacher is quite willing to affirm. 'We must conclude, then, that ideality is the only appropriate expression for the exclusive personal dignity of Christ' (93.2, p. 379).

The continuity of Jesus' person with natural human existence is stressed repeatedly in Schleiermacher's exposition. His birth and life are wholly natural phenomena. Miracles are not required to explain his person. 'The appearance of the Redeemer in history is, as divine revelation, neither an absolutely supernatural nor an absolutely supra-rational thing' (13, p. 62). His life of communion with God and his experience of blessedness lie, in Schleiermacher's thought, wholly within the realm of human possibilities:

> But notwithstanding, it must be asserted that even the most rigorous view of the difference between Him and all other men does not hinder us from saying that His appearing, even regarded as the incarnation of the Son of God, is a natural fact. For in the first place: as certainly as Christ was a man, there must reside in human nature the possibility of taking up the divine into itself, just as did happen in Christ. So that the idea that the divine revelation in Christ must in this respect be something absolutely supernatural will simply not stand the test. (13.1, p. 64)

And yet in Schleiermacher's Christology there does appear to be something absolutely different about the nature of Jesus' piety. It has to with its origin. Whereas the God-consciousness and blessedness of all Christians is derived from him, Jesus has these in himself. This it would seem is the one absolutely differentiating characteristic of his person – his God-consciousness is not derived from his community or antecedents. Rather, he has this blessedness independently of the people of faith and is able to communicate it directly to others. And this is perhaps all that is entailed by Jesus' particular dignity or divinity, as the word is sometimes loosely employed in Schleiermacher's exposition. For, according to him, it is unnecessary to afford Jesus a higher status than that which is required for him to accomplish his redemptive ministry.

> So that it is vain to attribute to the Redeemer a higher dignity than the activity at the same time ascribed to Him demands, since nothing is explained by this surplus of dignity. (92.2, p. 375)

We turn them to the nature of Christ's saving work. How does he redeem his people? Whether or not one agrees with Schleiermacher's theological project, the persuasive simplicity of his twofold response is brilliantly conceived:

> The Redeemer assumes believers into the power of His God-consciousness, and this is His redemptive activity. (100, p. 425)
> The Redeemer assumes the believers into the fellowship of His unclouded blessedness, and this is His reconciling activity. (101, p. 431)

The principal characteristic of redemption is, for Schleiermacher, the removal of sin and this is identical in his thought with the restoration of God-consciousness. The complementary concept of reconciliation he understands as sharing in the unclouded blessedness of Christ, where there is no consciousness of evil and consequently where any consciousness of deserving punishment comes to an end.

THE COMMUNICATION OF SALVATION

How does the believer come to share in the blessedness of Christ and so experience redemption? Schleiermacher proposes that salvation is mediated through the community of faith. It is in this community which goes back to the one which originally formed around Jesus that 'redemption is effected by Him through the communication of His sinless perfection' (88, p. 361).

The ongoing church is, Schleiermacher argues, the causal historical chain that links modern believers to the person of Christ. By the self-presentation of his own blessedness through his words and actions Jesus initially attracted a community of disciples and made them one with himself. This first community's experience of Jesus was unmediated. Schleiermacher argues that: 'If we start from the principle that our Christianity ought to be the same as the Apostles, our Christianity too must have been generated by the personal influence of Christ . . . These influences cannot now emanate from him directly' (127.2, p. 587). Nervous of any form of supernaturalism Schleiermacher is unwilling to allow the direct action of the Holy Spirit as a way of explaining the personal influence of Christ on succeeding generations.

> If faith arises in the same way, conversion must happen in the same way. Now in the first disciples both were affected by the Word in its widest sense, that is, by the whole prophetic activity of Christ. And we must be able to understand this that we have in common with them if need be without a doctrine of the Holy Spirit, just as the disciples understood their own condition without any such doctrine. The constant factor is above all the divine power of the Word – taking the expression in its widest sense – by which conversion is still effected and faith still arises. (108.5, p. 490)

The personal influence of Christ is mediated through the ongoing community of faith which continues to hold, as it were, a picture of Jesus, a picture constructed from his words and actions as recorded in the Gospels and New Testament witness. There is nothing supernatural in Christ's present influence, rather it 'consists solely in the human communication of the Word, in so far as that communication embodies Christ's word and continues the indwelling divine power of Christ Himself' (108.5, p. 492). Schleiermacher concludes his argument:

> [T]he individual even today receives from the picture of Christ, which exists in the community as at once corporate act and a corporate possession, the impression of the sinless perfection of Jesus, which becomes for him at the same time the perfect consciousness of sin and the removal of the misery. (88.3, p. 364)

Why is Schleiermacher so careful to construct a model of salvation that is mediated by the Christian community? It is his alternative to what he terms a 'magical' view of the atonement, an interpretation of Christ's saving work which could be applied in somewhat different ways to all four of the theologians whose work has been discussed in the preceding chapters.

A MAGICAL VIEW OF SALVATION

Many of those living under the influence of the Enlightenment believed that the supernaturalism associated with the theology of an earlier age had been discredited by the advance of science. Further, interpretations of the atonement in terms of vicarious satisfaction – that Jesus paid for our sins – had come to be considered as morally problematic in certain circles. Schleiermacher shared both these concerns and believed that supernaturalism and substitutionary views of the atonement were closely related and used the pejorative expression 'magical' to describe them.

> Only those views of Christ's reconciling activity appear to be magical which make the impartation of His blessedness independent of assumption into vital fellowship with Him. This means that the forgiveness of sins is made to depend upon the punishment which Christ suffered, and the blessedness of men itself is presented as a reward which God offers to Christ for the suffering of that punishment. (101.3, p. 435)

Schleiermacher's theory that Christ's reconciling activity is effective only through his assumption of believers into a vital fellowship with himself appears to be the same as Calvin's argument that all the benefits a believer experiences come through his or her union with Christ. Schleiermacher's concern is, however, somewhat different. As scientists struggled to understand how one body could act upon another at a distance, as the theory of gravitation requires, so Schleiermacher could not conceive how the atonement, an event in the first century, could influence a person's present relation with God other than through the natural mediation of an ongoing historic community.

> Now to warn those who lean to the side of magic, this touchstone must be kept before them, whether their conception really agrees with the possibility of conceiving the effective influence of Christ under this historical natural form. (101.4, p. 438)

Now this idea of the necessity of mediation is a useful tool for Schleiermacher in his opposition to what are now described as objective views of the atonement. Those who believe that something was achieved through Christ's death that radically affects the present relation between God and his people are proposing that an historical event can have a direct influence on us quite apart from any natural mediation across the time gap.

Schleiermacher is also deeply concerned about the moral implications arising from traditional views of the atonement. He cannot, for instance, conceive how the punishment of another might remove the feeling that one still deserves to be punished. The ethical concern remains.

> In no less a magical way is the forgiveness of sins achieved, if the consciousness of deserving punishment is supposed to cease because the punishment has been borne by another. That in this way the expectation of punishment might be taken away is conceivable; but this is merely the sensuous element in the forgiveness of sins. The properly ethical element, the consciousness of deserving punishment would still remain. (101.3, p. 435)

Although Schleiermacher's intention is to construct a systematic theology that maintains the outward form of classical Protestant dogmatics he struggles to find any grounds for holding that Jesus' death is in any way significant for our salvation.

> Least of all is it proper to ascribe such a special reconciling value to His physical sufferings; and that for two reasons. On the one hand, these sufferings in themselves have only the loosest connexion with His reaction against sin. On the other hand, our own experience teaches us that an ordinary ethical development and robust piety have as their reward the almost complete overcoming of physical sufferings in the presence of a glad spiritual self-consciousness, whether personal or corporate. (101.4, p. 437)

We should not be surprised then that with a quite different view of the human predicament and an unwillingness to recognize any redemptive efficacy to Christ's death, Schleiermacher's understanding of justification is not substantially continuous with the broad tradition of the Western Church.

JUSTIFICATION

Schleiermacher was a Lutheran theologian and justification was the central and determinative feature of his religious communion. It was the theological rationale for its breach with the Catholic Church, and so the distinguishing historical mark of its faith. If Schleiermacher was to put his theology forward as a faithful development of Protestant dogmatics he would have to define justification in terms which were in harmony with the Lutheran and Reformed confessions of faith. Here then is his definition:

> God's justifying of one who is converted to Him includes the forgiving of his sins, and the recognizing of him as a child of God. This transformation of his relation to God, however, follows only in so far as he has true faith in the Redeemer. (109, p. 496)

Although this appears to be in general agreement with the tradition a number of differences come to light as he expounds the doctrine. First, Schleiermacher means something quite different from what is normally understood by 'the forgiveness of sins'.

> In the common life of sinfulness the individual as a human being has no other relation to God except . . . a consciousness of being guilty before Him and meriting punishment. It is obvious this consciousness must cease as soon as through and along with faith living fellowship with Christ begins. (109.2, p. 498)

Forgiveness is not about what God himself does in an act of divine mercy. It has to do, rather, with an aspect of the consciousness of the believer as he or she enters a new relation with God. Why then should there no longer be any consciousness of guilt or sense of deserving of punishment in this new relationship? This is quite difficult for Schleiermacher to explain:

> The new man thus no longer takes sin to be his own; he indeed labours against it as something foreign to him. The consciousness of guilt is thus abolished. His penal desert must vanish with this. (109.2, pp. 498, 499)

Somehow, the new believer's battle with sin as an alien feature of his or her life removes any consciousness of guilt and penal desert. One might say forgiveness is a religious feeling I have through the examination of my own battle with sin at the outset of my new relation to God. It has its source in Christ in that through his influence I have come to this new consciousness of God. But is has nothing to do with his death on the cross or his fulfilment of the divine law or of his intercessions. At the end of the day forgiveness is something I glean from my own experience of sin in my new relation with God.

Further, the justifying decision of God is not about grace or mercy but has to do only with power.

> For the decision as to who is to attain to conversion and when we have already assigned, not the realm of grace, making it depend on Christ, but the realm of power, making it depend on God; which is the Father's drawing men to the Son. (109.3, pp. 500, 501)

Justification is also not strictly speaking a decision about that occurs in time, for God is not temporally conditioned as we are. Rather, '[t]here is only one eternal and universal decree justifying men for Christ's sake' (109.3, p. 501). Viewed subjectively, however, 'it is quite right to say that every act of conversion is for the man himself a declaration of the universal divine decree to justify for Christ's sake' (109.3, p. 503).

The outward shape of a Protestant understanding of justification is present in Schleiermacher's presentation. But the heart of it has been removed.

CONCLUSION

Schleiermacher's theological project must be judged first of all within the context of his time. It was undoubtedly a brilliant and bold attempt to represent the Christian faith in the intellectual world of the Enlightenment by conceiving of theology as the examination of the subject of that faith rather than its object.

How does one judge its success? It was well-received in the literary classes at the time and was certainly the most significant force in the shaping of nineteenth-century German liberalism. Its legacy survives in the religious ideas and perceptions of countless Christians today who might never have even heard of Schleiermacher's name let alone read *The Christian Faith* and yet feel somewhat at odds with the more objective, supernaturalist theology of traditional Christianity. But was his theology faithful to its subject-matter? Did it adequately present the gospel? Karl Barth the subject of our next chapter was convinced that it did not. We will in due course consider his response to it.

As to Schleiermacher's contribution to the doctrine of justification in Western theology I think it is fair to say that after him it was no longer possible to conceive of justification as the principal way of conceiving God's saving action in Christ, at least among the extensive community influenced by his thought. First, it radically undermined the idea of God as the awesome judge of all our thoughts, words and actions, as the one who in the objective and absolute holiness of his being stands over against our wickedness. Consequently, *his* free act of forgiveness was not seen as a necessary component of our salvation. Second, Schleiermacher's focus on the subjective element in the divine–human relationship meant that the concept of forgiveness was interpreted by him as an aspect of human piety rather than as the gracious act of the divine will. Forgiveness was viewed as a process that takes place wholly in human consciousness rather than one that has to do with the volition of God. Third, Christ's suffering and death, according to Schleiermacher, have no bearing on the matter of forgiveness.

Now as the merciful action of God and the efficacy of Christ's death in the forgiveness of our sins have always been essential features of the Western Church's doctrine of justification, one can understand why justification has come to be viewed as theologically peripheral among those shaped by Schleiermacher's thought.

Richard Niebuhr's critique of American religious liberalism in the early twentieth century could be applied with some accuracy to the soteriology of the great German theologian who was its most significant influence.

> A God without wrath brought men without sin into a kingdom without judgement through the ministrations of a Christ without a Cross.[4]

The religious framework within which a doctrine of justification operates had been effectively dismantled.

CHAPTER 8

KARL BARTH

A CRITIQUE OF SCHLEIERMACHER

The mindless devastation and unprecedented loss of life resulting from the First World War radically undermined the optimism in human possibilities that was the hallmark of German religious liberalism. A radical new breed of theologians came to the fore, including men like Karl Barth and Emil Brunner. Sensitive to the angst of their times, they argued that God had brought about a crisis, a turning point in history, which demanded a personal decision in the face of the inherent contradictions in the social order and human condition. It was to be a decision for or against God, a decision for life or for death.

The programme of these 'crisis' or 'neo-orthodox' theologians was, broadly speaking, to provide an alternative to the liberalism of the age with an imaginative re-presentation of Reformed theology. Barth recognized that the thought of Friedrich Schleiermacher lay behind the prevailing religious outlook and sought to provide an alternative theological world-view. In due course, he also offered a penetrating critique of Schleiermacher's principal work, *The Christian Faith.* Here are some of its main features.

First, Barth detected in Schleiermacher's theology an abiding desire to seek peace through moderation. Shaped by the influence of the Moravians and the Romantics, Schleiermacher's tendency was always to look for the uniting vision, the synthesis, the solution that lay somewhere between the extremes. Barth perceived that he was

zealous in attacking everything which can divide the Church, or which can set the individual hearer at loggerheads with himself, because it calls to mind the idea of irreconcilable contradictions. There are no such irreconcilable contradictions and therefore there cannot and may not be any unpeaceful state either in general or in particular, outwardly or inwardly. (*Protestant Theology in the Nineteenth Century*, p. 437)[1]

For Schleiermacher there is a relative nature about opposites and their quality as opposites is inevitably provisional. The truth always lies somewhere in the middle. By giving emphasis to pious self-awareness as the foundation of theological thought, intellectual truth or dogma, and the polarization of ideas that it so often leads to, is relegated to a secondary role. 'That is why for Schleiermacher proclaiming God means proclaiming one's own piety, that is why for him preaching consists essentially in self-imparting by the preacher' (p. 440). Nobody can argue with the facts of personal witness. Barth recognized that within such a perspective Christian doctrine becomes no more than 'the representation of the opinion of the Church' in a particular context and at a particular time.

Second, Barth was critical of Schleiermacher for assuming the role of an apologist in his exposition of Christian doctrine, believing that such a function was out of step with his primary duty as a theologian, that is, to offer a coherent exposition of the Word of God or gospel. In contrast to the work of the theologian Barth understood apologetics as 'an attempt to show . . . that the determining principles of philosophy and of historical and natural research . . . do not preclude, even if they do not directly require, the tenets of theology, which are founded upon revelation and upon faith respectively' (pp. 425, 426). The nature of the apologist's task implied, for Barth, that the one engaging in it had chosen to inhabit some neutral or higher ground in order to mediate between these two worlds of thought. In Schleiermacher's case that superior vantage point was his expertise in the science of the mind. From there he makes the deduction that religion is a necessary manifestation of human intellectual life and that Christianity is the highest form of religion. Such a higher position of vantage, one which stands apart from and external to Christianity is, according to Barth, a distorting and inadequate base for expounding a religion established by divine revelation.

Third, Schleiermacher succumbed to the anthropocentric spirit of the age by constructing his theology around the analysis of human piety. 'The great formal principle of Schleiermacher's theology is at the same time its material principle. Christian pious self-awareness contemplates and describes itself: this is in principle the be-all and end-all of his theology' (p. 443). Barth believed that having chosen the analysis of human piety as his fundamental theological principle Schleiermacher was bound to have difficulty in affirming the divine status of the historical person of Jesus Christ. His system of thought did not have the necessary conceptual structure to show how the historical element of Christianity was more than a temporal vehicle of timeless, reasonable truth. Although he recognizes that Schleiermacher did have a brilliantly conceived Christology based on the concept of mediation that is both modern and in keeping with his theological project, Barth argued that Schleiermacher does not establish Jesus Christ to be God in the only sure way his system conceives of God, that is, as the one on whom we are absolutely dependent.

How then was Barth to respond to Schleiermacher? He quotes H. Scholz's comment on *The Christian Faith* with approval: 'Schleiermacher did not succeed in everything; but his achievement as a whole is so great, that the only threat to it would be a corresponding counter-achievement, not a cavilling criticism of detail' (p. 413). It would appear that Barth came to recognize that the production of such 'a corresponding counter-achievement' was the particular task that had fallen to him. That is why his own critique of Schleiermacher is so interesting – it indicates the perspectives that were to shape his own massive theological scheme, one that he almost managed to bring to completion in the 13 volumes of the *Church Dogmatics.*

A RESPONSE TO LIBERALISM

At the outbreak of the First World War a number of Barth's teachers signed a declaration in support of the Kaiser. This led to his own deep personal disillusionment with the theology that had shaped his academic formation. John Webster quotes a fascinating autobiographical fragment indicating Barth's theological intention.

By 1916 a number of us of the younger theological generation had hesitantly set out to introduce a theology better than that of the nineteenth century and of the turn of the century – better in

JUSTIFICATION: A GUIDE FOR THE PERPLEXED

the sense that in it, God, in his unique position over against man, and especially religious man, might be clearly given the honour we found him to have in the Bible.[2]

The first salvo of his response to the prevailing liberal theology came in 1918 with the publication of his provocative commentary on Romans. As could be expected there was on outcry against the book. In the preface to the second edition of 1921 he considered the charge levelled against him by his critics that his radical new presentation of Reformed orthodoxy had been shaped by a system.

> My reply is that, if I have as system, it is limited to a recognition of what Kierkegaard called the 'infinite qualitative distinction' between time and eternity, and to my regarding this as possessing negative as well as positive significance: 'God is in heaven and thou are on earth.' The relation between such a God and such a man and the relation between such a man and such a God, is for me the theme of the Bible and the essence of philosophy. (p. 10)

Whereas Schleiermacher had sought to find a synthesis between opposing positions and the resolution of polarities, Barth delighted to emphasize the disjunction between time and eternity, between God and humankind. This meant that his use of paradox in the presentation of his dogmatics was not so much a quirk of his writing or preaching style but rather the form that he believed was required by the subject-matter. A dialectic theology in which opposing views were held together was required in order to express adequately the infinite qualitative distinction between heaven and earth and the far-reaching implications of this. Those who would read Barth, particularly his earlier work, have to come to terms with this paradoxical and often very creative way of writing where contrary ideas are held together boldly rather than being brought into a coherent synthesis through modification or qualification. There is, however, a fine line between paradox and incoherence and even his supporters have to concede that this line was sometimes crossed.

Second, Barth sought to find the interpretative foundation for theology not as Schleiermacher did in the science of the mind or from some other intellectual vantage point external to the Christian faith, but from within the gospel itself. Barth's early summary of salvation takes this twofold form. God speaks to man. God enables

112

man to hear him speak. The divine speech-act to man is the Word
of God, the divine enablement of humans to hear and respond to
that Word is the Holy Spirit. A decisive element in this analysis
of divine salvation is that the Word of God and the Holy Spirit
are conceived of as actions. According to Barth, we encounter the
Word of God, this divine speech-act not immediately or directly
but in one of three created forms – in Jesus Christ, in the scriptures
and in the preaching of the gospel. Barth goes further: 'Revelation
does not differ from the person of Jesus Christ nor from the reconciliation accomplished in Him' (I.1.4.3, p. 119). This unqualified
identification of the Word of God, understood as a divine revelatory action, with both the person of Jesus Christ and his saving
mission is important for Barth, but also quite difficult for many
students, including this one, to get their heads around. A confusion
of categories appears to be taking place. Persons, actions and out-
comes are boldly identified with one another, but they are clearly
not the same sort of things. You cannot, for instance, nail an action
to a cross. Barth does not always slow down and explain how paradoxical identifications such as these, however, illuminating, are to
be qualified so that they actually make sense.

Third, Barth's concept of saving revelation implies a quite different Trinitarian conceptuality from that of the tradition. The
student who would understand Barth here must 'put on hold'
their perception of God as three divine persons in intimate relation to one another who share in one common being, and try and
try and conceive of him as three divine modes of being – Revealer,
Revelation and Revealedness. The doctrine of God is, he argued,
to be formed from an analysis of the self-authenticating reality
of divine revelation,[3] rather than through a process of abstract
speculation derived from a world of ideas that stand apart from
or external to God's saving action. Further, by constructing his
dogmatics in this manner, the divinity of Jesus Christ is ensured
from the outset. According to Barth, only God can reveal God. As
the self-revelation of God, Jesus Christ is himself divine. We find
then in Barth's theology a God who stands in freedom over against
humankind, infinitely and qualitatively distinct from it, a God who
through his saving revelation is manifest in three modes of being.

In summary, while Schleiermacher's theological style was
conciliatory in its tendency, always searching for the balanced
middle-position, Barth's was dialectical, delighting in holding

opposites together and emphasizing the absolute distinction between God and humankind. Whereas Schleiermacher began his systematic theology from a study of human consciousness and deduced from there the possibility of religion, Barth sought to establish his key interpretative principles from the reality of the gospel. Finally while Schleiermacher's Christology was constructed from 'below', from human religious self-awareness, Barth's Christology was derived from 'above' from the givenness of divine self-revelation and the identification of Jesus Christ with the divine revelatory act.

Within a theology generated by these principles how did Barth understand the salvation of humankind?

THE ELECTION OF THE SON

One of Barth's most significant acts of theological innovation was to make the doctrine of election both the basis of his exposition of salvation and a central feature in his doctrine of God.

> The doctrine of election is the sum of the Gospel because of all words that can be said or heard it is the best: that God elects man . . . It is part of the doctrine of God because originally God's election of man is a predestination not merely of man but of Himself. (II.2.32, p. 3)

For Barth, the person of Jesus Christ lies at the heart of the doctrine of salvation not only in that he is the instrument of God's redemptive purpose who suffers judgement in our stead, but also and principally because he is the object of God's saving love. God first chooses his Son. Our salvation is derivative in the sense that it is ours only as we are caught up in God's eternal choice of his Son. 'In Him God's plan for man is disclosed, God's judgment on man fulfilled, God's deliverance of man accomplished, God's gift to man present in fullness, God's claim and promise to man declared' (II.2.33.1, p. 94). The election of the Son is the first great choice of God made at the beginning of time:

> He is the election of God before which and without which and beside which God cannot make any other choices. (II.2.33.1, p. 94)

All that needs to be said of God's response to humankind is included in the election of the Son. In it is the dark and terrible judgement on our human sin, in it is our election to life eternal. 'It is in Him that the eternal election becomes immediately and directly the promise of our own election as it is enacted in time, our calling, our summoning to faith, our assent to the divine intervention on our behalf . . . the communication of the Holy Spirit' (II.2.33.1, pp. 105, 106). Each constituent element in the salvation of humankind is already determined in the election of the Son. The way God deals with us is simply part and parcel of what has already taken place in the way he has dealt with his Son.

The eternal election of Jesus Christ, however, is not merely a divine choice that resolves every facet of the salvation of men and women. It is also a decision that constitutes the very nature and being of God. God chooses to be a God with a particular commitment to the salvation of men and women; he chooses to be a God for them, taking up their lost cause. It is an orientation that determines his own being. The election of Jesus means the decision of God to have the Word alongside himself. 'What choice can precede the choice by which God has of Himself chosen to have with Himself in the beginning of all things the Word which is Jesus?' (II.2.33.1, pp. 100, 101). The Trinitarian nature of God is consequently an outcome of a free and sovereign decision of God.

> Are we not forced to say that the electing consists in this Word and decree in the beginning; and conversely, that this Word and decree in the beginning are God's electing, His free, subjective self-determination, the primal act of lordship over everything else, independently of all outward constraint, conditioning or compulsion? (II.2.33.1, p. 100)

The claim that the Word of God comes to be by the free self-determining choice of God, made not eternally but at the beginning of creation,[4] is a momentous one. It is significant for the Church because this question of the origin of the Son gave rise to the most decisive theological debate in its long history. The Arians argued for the primacy of God's will among the divine attributes and held that the Word or Son of God was a product of the divine volition at the beginning of creation. He was not eternal. He was rather brought into being so that as God's Word he might be his instrument for the creation of humankind. 'Then wishing to form us, thereupon He made a certain one, and named him Word and Wisdom and Son, that he might form us by means of Him.'[5] This idea was viewed as highly problematic by Athanasius who recognized that if the Son was a product of the divine will, he came into existence by a creative decision of God, in much the same way as the rest of the universe. Against such a view he argued that the Son was derived not from the Father's will but from his being. The Arians, holding as they did to the priority of divine freedom, challenged his position claiming: 'Unless He has by will come to be, therefore God had a Son by necessity and against His good pleasure.'[6] Athanasius responded: 'As far as then as the Son transcends the creature, by so much then does what is by nature transcend the will.'[7]

The decision taken at the Council of Nicea to promulgate the doctrine that the Son was of one substance with the Father signalled the triumph of Athanasius' argument that the existence of the Son was derived from the Father by nature and not by will. By making the doctrine of election a principal aspect of his doctrine of God, Barth is proposing a significant modification of one of the central pillars of Christian theological thought.

When Barth speaks of the election of God's Word in the beginning, and the consequent determination of the triune being of God, to whom precisely is he referring? Is it the eternal Son or is it that Son incarnated as Jesus Christ, a divine–human person? The tradition has always allowed a distinction to be made between the *logos asarkos*, the Word unenfleshed and that same Word as he took to himself a human nature. This is not a distinction that Barth was generally willing to concede.

> The first and eternal Word of God, which underlies and precedes the creative will and work as the beginning of all things in God, means in fact Jesus Christ . . . In this context we must not refer to the 'second' person of the Trinity as such, to the eternal Son or the eternal Word of God *in abstracto*, and therefore to the so-called *logos asarkos*. (IV.1, pp. 51, 52)

In the context of God's redemptive action Barth finds no place in theological reflection for the divine Word of God abstracted or separated from his human nature. To those shaped by the logic of traditional Trinitarian thought this seems to be a strange and radical restriction. In an attempt to protect Barth from a charge of incoherence Bruce McCormack argues that he does in fact allow the reality of the unenfleshed divine Logos as *incarnandus*,[8] that is, as the one who existed apart from the flesh but who would in due course be incarnated. But this is not a differentiation that Barth here or elsewhere makes and it undermines the development of his ideas in the pages that follow. If we are to understand his thought we must take seriously his refusal to allow in the economy of salvation any role to be given to the eternal Word of God *in abstracto*, rather than to the Word as incarnate.

Who then is the elected Word of God? According to Barth the Word of God, who was elected to be with God at the very beginning is Jesus himself. It is not a divine person who would in time become Jesus. In his exposition of the prologue to John's Gospel he argues: 'In John1:1 the reference is very clear: *ho logos* is unmistakeably substituted for Jesus . . . It is He, Jesus who is in the beginning with God. It is He who by nature is God' (II.2.33.1, p. 96). But in what sense is Jesus, the God-man present with God at the very beginning?

> We can and must say that Jesus Christ was in the beginning with God in the sense that all creation and its history was in God's plan and decree with God. But he was so not merely in this way. He was also in the beginning with God as 'the first born of every creature' (Col1:15), Himself the plan and decree of God, Himself the divine decision with respect to all creation and its history whose content is already determined. (II.2.33.1, p. 104)

Barth is not suggesting that a person with a human body and mind was with God from eternity. He is saying that Jesus is the first decision of God, his foundational decree, his primal choice and it is in this sense, as this verbal decision, he is with God from the beginning of his creative work and is consequently determinative of God's Trinitarian being.

How then is the reconciliation of humankind, decreed and determined in the choice of Jesus from eternity, worked out in our time and history?

THE DOCTRINE OF RECONCILIATION

A student might feel somewhat overwhelmed and intimidated when confronted by the sheer volume of Barth's writing on the doctrine of reconciliation. However, in a section of about 150 pages in the *Church Dogmatics* (chapters 57, 58 of IV.1) he provides a lucid summary of his exposition of the doctrine, highlighting all of its principal features. I will use this as the basic text in our discussion below.

Barth's soteriological model is shaped for the most part by the theology of Luther and Calvin. But he handles this Reformed tradition with an imaginative freedom, transforming a number of its features. Some of these modifications are of particular significance for the way his soteriology functions as a structure for the defence and the presentation of the gospel. Let us look then at the principal elements of his doctrine of reconciliation.

Barth viewed sin not simply as the absence of the good in the mode of Augustine, but rather as a non-substantial, alien intrusion into God's good creation, an invasion that is always finally subject to the sovereign will and purpose.

> It (sin) has its being only in the fact that it is non-being, that which from the point of view of God is unintelligible and intolerable. It takes place only as the powerful but, of course, before God absolutely powerless irruption of that which is not into the fulfilment of His will. It takes place, therefore, only under the original, radical, definitive and therefore finally triumphant No of God. (IV.1.57.2, p. 46)

What is of particular significance in Barth's view of our knowledge of sin is that he holds that sin is not discovered from the human conscience or from the transgression of the law as such, but only from within the experience of redemption. It is from Jesus Christ that we learn the nature of sin. Barth thereby subverts the traditional understanding of the epistemic direction of the Spirit's gracious work, that is, from the hearing of the law, to a knowledge of sin, to a discovery of God's mercy in Christ. For him the direction is reversed and flows back from salvation in Christ to a recognition of sin and the true meaning of the law. Sin is a denial of grace, a breach of the covenant which can be known only in the light of the experience of grace.

What according to Barth is the ultimate consequence of human sin? What is the human predicament?

By sin man puts himself in the wrong in relation to God. He makes himself impossible as the creature and covenant-partner of God. He desecrates the good nature which has been given and forfeits the grace which is addressed to him. He compromises his existence. For he has no right as a sinner. He is only in the wrong. (IV.1.61.2, p. 528)

As such sinful man stands under the wrath of God. Barth is loathe, however, to pause here and consider the implications of the human condition apart from its resolution in Christ. 'We cannot speak of the being of man except from the standpoint of the Christian and in the light of the particular being of man in Jesus Christ' (IV.1.58.2, p. 92). Salvation from our human plight is, according to Barth, accomplished in the death of Jesus. To explain the efficacy of Christ's death he employs what might be called a mediatorial model of the atonement whereby Christ lives and dies as the representative human who comes under divine judgement in the stead of sinful man.

In his place Jesus Christ has suffered the death of a malefactor. The sentence on him as a sinner has been carried out. It cannot be reversed. It does not need to be repeated. It has fallen instead on Jesus Christ. In and with the man who was taken down dead on Golgotha man the covenant-breaker is buried and destroyed. He has ceased to be. The wrath of God which is the fire of His love has taken him away and all his transgressions and offences and errors and follies and lies and faults and crimes against God and his fellowmen and himself, just as a whole burnt offering is consumed on the altar with the flesh and skin and bones and hoofs and horns, rising up as fire to heaven and disappearing. (IV.1.58.2, pp. 93–94)

Jesus' priestly role as Mediator, that is, his offering of himself as a sacrifice for human sinfulness is referred by Barth to his divine nature. It is the central element in his exposition of what the Mediator does for our salvation as very God.

He is God in the fact that He can give Himself up and does give Himself up not merely to the creaturely limitation but to the suffering of the human creature, becoming one of these men, Himself bearing the judgment under which they stand, willing to die and, in fact, dying the death which they have deserved. (IV.1.58.4, p. 130)

Reformed theology, particularly, as it is found in the work of John Calvin, refers this priestly ministry to Jesus' human nature. Developing the argument of the letter to the Hebrews it recognizes that to be a faithful high priest Jesus had to be like one of us, he had to be a true human, physically sharing in our ancestry, tempted as we are and suffering as we do. Why does Barth transpose the tradition, and it would seem the scriptures, in this manner and refer the priestly service of Jesus to his divinity, to Jesus as God rather than to Jesus as man?

At the beginning of the *Church Dogmatics* Barth identified Jesus Christ with the act of divine revelation and the reconciliation of humankind. 'Revelation does not differ from the person of Jesus Christ nor from the reconciliation accomplished in Him' (I.1.4.3, p. 119). Twenty years further on when he comes to expound the doctrine of reconciliation, the idea of revelation is no longer a central feature of his presentation of salvation, nevertheless, Barth continues to hold fast to the idea that the saving event of Jesus' suffering and death is a divine act. Perhaps he feels compelled to do so to protect the divinity of Christ, for he has always identified the act and the person. But how is he able to explain the notion that God performs what is clearly a human role? He does so with the concept of kenosis or divine humiliation whereby God empties himself: 'in Jesus Christ God – we do not say casts off his Godhead but (as the One who loves in sovereign freedom) activates and proves it by the fact that He gives Himself to the limitation and suffering of the human creature' (IV.1.58.4, p. 134). This is a highly problematic way of proceeding, particularly, for one who introduced his theological project by arguing that there is an infinite qualitative distinction between God and man. It seems to me that it is wiser here to be disciplined by the strictures of the Definition of Chalcedon. The divine and human natures are not to be confused. They are not changeable. One cannot simply perform the actions of the other. God in his own being does not by an act of the will morph into a human way of behaving, the mistaken notion of Doceticism. That is why the incarnation is so important – the Word needed to become incarnate, that is, to take to himself a human nature so that as a *man* he might live, suffer and die for his fellow men and women.

How is this salvation, accomplished in the life and death of Jesus, applied to God's covenant people?

JUSTIFICATION

Barth carefully lays out the framework underlying his understanding of justification. One of its key concepts is that of the righteousness of God. 'The right of God established in the death of Jesus Christ, and proclaimed in his resurrection in defiance of the wrong of man is the basis of the new and corresponding right of man' (IV.1.61, p. 514). Taking an independent position from the Reformers and nearly all the doctors of the ancient Church, Barth argues that the right or righteousness of God is not the reconciled state of the believer that God brings about, a righteousness that comes from God, but rather the manifest justice of God in the justification of men and women. God's righteousness in his justifying judgement is not to be determined by some higher law but by his own being: 'Not subject to any alien law, but Himself the origin and basis and revealer of all true law, He is just in Himself' (IV.1.61.2, pp. 530, 531). What was accomplished in Christ's death, proclaimed in the resurrection and make effective for men and women is just or righteous because God himself is eternally just. The inherent justice of his justifying decree is what Barth means by the righteousness of God.

In contrast to the righteousness of God, humans are unrighteous, they have alienated themselves from God, made him their enemy and brought upon themselves his holy wrath. But the deep wrong of renegade man does not overthrow the righteousness of God or the divine determination of his life. 'He has not escaped the right of God over him and to him, but is still subject to it, utterly and completely. He is still in the sphere of God's jurisdiction' (IV.1.61.2, p. 534).

The justifying judgement of God brings about a new righteousness in sinful men and women. What is the nature of this new righteousness? It is at its heart the forgiveness of sins. Here Barth is completely at one with the tradition.

Pardon – by God and therefore unconditionally pronounced and unconditionally valid – that is man's justification. In the judgement of God, according to His election and rejection, there is made in the midst of time, and as the central event of all human history, referring to all the men who live both before and after, a decision, a divisive sentence. Its result – expressed in the death and resurrection of Jesus Christ – is the pardon of sins. (IV.1.61.3, p. 568)

What is striking in Barth's exposition of justification is the universal nature of this pardon. Man is justified whether or not he knows of or responds to the divine pardon: 'Whether man hears it, whether he accepts it and lives as one who is pardoned is another question' (IV.1.61.3, p. 568). Does this mean that Barth is a universalist? In short, does he hold that other than Jesus Christ on the cross, no man or women will ever experience rejection and suffer the final damning judgement of God?

In his discussion on election Barth does make a clear distinction between individuals who are elected by God and those who are rejected: 'the rejected man is from the outset and in all circumstances quite other than the elect. He is the man who is *not* willed by the almighty, holy and compassionate God' (II.2.35.4, p. 450). But invariably in his reflections on this matter Barth indicates that even the rejected cannot continue as such. 'By permitting the life of a rejected man to be the life of his own Son, God has made such a life objectively impossible for all others' (II.2.35.2, p. 346). Why does Barth so struggle to allow the final rejection of the rejected even when faced with arguments that appear to demand it? It has to do, I believe, with the whole structure of his soteriology.

First, in the election of his Son, God's determines to be a God for us, to take up our lost cause as his own. The election of Jesus is the primal choice that transforms the nature of God's own being. The ongoing reality of rejected men and women appears, in the light of this momentous original election of the Word of God, to be a denial of the very being of the triune God. Second, if the nature of sin is viewed in relation to God as a powerless irruption of that which is not; if contrary to its own intention, it brings into effect the divine will; then it is difficult to conceive how sin might finally triumph in the life of an individual and successfully withstand the grace of God. Third, if the right of God by which God justifies the sinner has to do with his own inherent righteousness; if it is worked out in the death of Christ and demonstrated in his resurrection; if the wrong of man is insignificant in comparison with such righteousness; then it is hard to see how can human rebellion have the final say and remain outside the determination of God's ultimate right? Each of the main features of Barth's doctrine of reconciliation appears to require the ultimate triumph of God's righteousness over human sin and so the final salvation of all.

There are, however, a number of difficulties with the theory that all men and women of all times are pardoned by the one justifying judgement of God. The first has to do with the role of human faith in justification. Augustine's dictum: 'The justification of God can exist without your will, but it cannot exist in you without your willing it. Therefore he who made you without yourself does not justify you without yourself. He made you without your knowledge, but he justifies you only if you wish it'[9] is a reminder that the Church has long held that divine sovereignty in justification does not require human passivity. To recognize that human faith is an essential element in the event of justification is not to succumb to Pelagianism or to the view that humans contribute materially towards their own salvation. Faith, broadly understood as a looking to God for salvation and trusting in Jesus as God's covenantal promise is, according to Paul, the proper framework of grace. 'Therefore, the promise comes by faith, so that it may be by grace and may be guaranteed to all Abraham's offspring' (Rom. 4.16a). Faith is embedded in the Pauline doctrine of justification. It is closely related to salvation in all the Gospels. It has long been understood by the Church as the means by which the Holy Spirit applies to sinners the redemption accomplished in Christ. It cannot, therefore, be separated off from the act justification. Divine pardon cannot be abstracted from the responsive faith of the one who hears the gospel.

Secondly, Barth made a clear distinction between God's saving action in the wider world and in the Church:

To that extent, objectively, all are justified, sanctified and called. But the hand of God has not touched all in such a way that they can see and hear, perceive and accept and receive all that God is for all and therefore for them, how therefore they can exist and think and live . . . In this special sense Christians and only Christians are converted to Him. (IV.1.584, p. 148)

The particular ability of Christians to hear, accept and receive all that God has done is referred by Barth to the work of the Holy Spirit:

> [I]t is the Holy Spirit, the being and work of the one eternal God in this special form, that is still lacking in the world at large. That God did not owe His Son, and in that Son Himself, to the world, is revealed by the fact that He gives His Spirit to whom He will. (IV.1.58.4, p. 148)

God gives his Son to the whole world but his Spirit only to the Church. Only some of those who have been justified respond in joyful obedience and faith as they live out the implications of their calling. But these are surely intolerable distinctions. When God offers himself in covenant to be our God, he does so as Father, Son and Holy Spirit. The triune persons cannot be split apart in the covenantal promise. If we do not have the Spirit of Christ we do not have Christ. Further, justification cannot be detached from the life of obedient faith and love, the life of holiness. Those whom God justifies he will also sanctify.

Thirdly, if all men and women have been justified, sanctified and called then the salvation of which these terms speak has no value as such in this life. Such a salvation is clearly not a reality that reconciles rebels to God, that transforms hearts, opens eyes and sets prisoners free. If every member of this broken world who continues to live in open defiance of God is in fact already justified then the justifying judgement of itself accomplishes nothing in the present world of human existence. It is an empty word.

CONCLUSION

I suggested at the close of the last chapter that Richard Niebuhr's critique of American religious liberalism could be applied with some accuracy to the soteriology of Friedrich Schleiermacher: 'A God without wrath brought men without sin into a Kingdom without judgment through the ministrations of a Christ without a Cross.'[10] If this is the case, then Schleiermacher effectively dismantled the religious conceptual framework within which a doctrine of justification is meaningful.

Barth's theology can be viewed in some measure as a response to that of Schleiermacher. I believe it is fair to say that within modern religious thought he reconstructed a world of ideas which affirmed without qualification the wrath of God on human sinfulness manifest in his dreadful judgement of Jesus Christ on the cross. In short, he appeared to recreate the basic conditions necessary for a doctrine of justification.

His imaginative representation of Reformed theology does lead to some major divergences from classical Protestant interpretations of justification. First, he has committed God's being to the positive outcome of the lost cause of humankind in a way that does not fit well with Christ's role as the final judge of the world. The punishment of recalcitrant sinners appears to be an inappropriate task for one whose whole being is determined by his election to stand in the stead of those rejected. For those who have come under the influence of Barth, the raised armed of Christ on the Day of Judgement, brilliantly portrayed by Michelangelo in the Sistine Chapel, can only be viewed as a terrible misreading of Jesus' person and work. There is simply no space in Barth's scheme for the risen and ascended Christ to serve at the right hand of the God as his plenipotentiary who will return in glory to judge the living and the dead – a position which, as the Gospels repeatedly indicate, Jesus recognized as his own.

A second distinction flows from Barth's view that sin is only known from within the experience of grace. It means that Barth is able to announce to the world its pardon by God, before he explains the serious consequences of sin and why divine forgiveness is so important. Absolution is offered apart from contrition and confession. Peace is proclaimed to those who do not seek God's favour. Justification is held to apply to those who have not believed in Jesus. Such a presentation of the gospel effectively replaces the proper dynamic between preacher and hearer with a form of monologue in which the hearer plays no active part and it would seem does not even need to be present.

Finally, the wrath of God and his judgement against sin have been so effectively and universally borne by Jesus Christ in Barth's thought that it is difficult for the hearers of this message to take seriously any warning of divine judgement whatever evil they might be doing to their fellows. If the anger of God has been absolutely and finally dealt with in the condemning judgement of Jesus then the concept of God's holy opposition to sin made known in the law no longer serves any religious function, whether as a restraint on the tyranny of wrongdoing or as a schoolmaster that leads the awakened person to Christ.

It has been the theme of this book that the gospel as expressed in the message of justification makes sense only within a particular religious world-view, one in which men and women are aware that they stand guilty before the high judge of heaven and live estranged from God. The highly influential theology of Schleiermacher, and for quite different reasons that of Barth, undermined belief in the ongoing meaningfulness of that particular world-view and so, I would argue, played no small part in the general neglect of the doctrine of justification in the second half of the twentieth century.

There has, however, in recent years been a revival of interest in the subject of justification with the matter being approached from a wholly new perspective. We will consider the ideas of one of the leading proponents of this new way of looking at Paul's understanding of the concept of justification in the next chapter.

CHAPTER 9

A NEW PERSPECTIVE

JUSTIFICATION AND JUDGEMENT

For the past hundred years or so much of the Western Church has felt uncomfortable with its creedal confession of Christ as the coming judge of the living and the dead. It is not merely that belief in the Second Coming of Christ has been eroded. Rather the whole idea of men and women being required to a give an account of their lives before a righteous judge now seems inappropriate in the light of what many Christians have come to believe about the nature of God and his purpose for humankind. I have argued in the previous two chapters that Schleiermacher and Barth both played, in quite different ways, significant roles in this change of outlook. The human predicament now tends to be viewed as one or more of a number of threats to human well-being such as the destruction of the environment, the tyranny of oppressive regimes, the dangers of religious fundamentalism, the inevitability of sickness and ageing, personal addiction to destructive behavioural patterns and the intractable power of sin in human life. Standing one day as sinners before the judgement seat of a holy God is no longer widely considered as something we need to be unduly worried about.

The doctrine of justification in nearly all the forms we have considered is dependent on the notion that we are indeed accountable to God for our lives and that we find ourselves estranged from him because of our sins. With the dismantling of this understanding of the human predicament, the doctrine of justification has fallen into neglect and has been shifted to the periphery of theological attention for it no longer serves any useful religious function. However, in recent times there has been a remarkable renewal of interest in the subject. Numerous articles and books are being written on justification. Internet chat-rooms are alive with heated discussion about the precise meaning of long-neglected concepts like the 'righteousness of God'. Why has the matter again become a matter of intense debate? The answer is that justification is being interpreted in a quite new way. Significantly, it is an interpretation that is no longer dependent on understanding the human predicament in terms of personal accountability and estrangement from God.

How different is this new interpretation of justification from all that went before? It is suggested by Tom Wright, one of the leading voices in the movement that has come to be described as the 'New Perspective', that every theologian from Augustine to Barth has quite misunderstood what Paul had to say about the matter.

> The discussion of justification in much of the history of the church, certainly since Augustine, got off on the wrong foot – at least in understanding Paul – and they have stayed there ever since.[1]

This is a remarkably bold and sweeping statement. It is, however, the considered view of a number of respected scholars who share the belief that there is a viable way of understanding Paul that is quite different from the doctrine outlined in the preceding chapters. Within this new perspective, justification does not have anything to do with the resolution of the human predicament. It is in fact not about salvation at all. Rather, it has to do with being recognized as part of the church community.

> Justification in this setting, then, is not a matter of how someone enters the community of the true people of God, but of how you tell who belongs to that community . . . In standard Christian theological language, it wasn't so much about soteriology as about ecclesiology; not so much about salvation as about the church. (*What St Paul Really Said*, p. 119)

What brought about such a radical reassessment of the meaning of justification? What are the issues that have led many to abandon the old structures of Pauline interpretation?

NEW QUESTIONS

The comparative study of religions is concerned not so much with grounding, evaluating and systematizing religious truth claims, but in examining the role such claims play in the way religious communities function and structure themselves. It seeks, for instance, to understand the basis on which religions accept new members or expel those who are wayward; what the features are which distinguish their adherents from those of other religious groups; how those who breach the rules of their particular community can be reinstated and what concepts are used to understand transference into the community from outside. When a comparison was made between a theoretical community shaped only by Pauline thought and one that is characterized by what is known of Palestinian Judaism a whole range of new and interesting proposals emerge which challenge conclusions that have long been held in traditional Pauline scholarship.

The particular matter that lies at the heart of the new interpretation of justification has to do with the legalistic nature of Jewish religion. The traditional reading of Paul is that he viewed Jews in his day as seeking to establish their own righteousness rather than accepting God's free gift of righteousness in Christ. Paul, it was thought, believed that many Jews were caught up in a form of self-righteousness or legalism. E. T. Saunders, a leading scholar in the comparative study of religions, challenged such a view, arguing in his book *Paul and Palestinian Judaism*[2] that the evidence does not bear out the charge that the Jews of the day were trying to attain salvation by their own righteous acts. Palestinian Judaism when carefully examined was not an essentially legalistic religion at all. It was rather a form of 'covenantal nomism', a religious system which exhibited a proper relation between grace and law in ways that are not too dissimilar from that which is found in Christianity. Speaking of Palestinian Judaism Saunders held that: 'in all the literature surveyed, *obedience maintains one's position in the covenant, but it does not earn God's grace as such*. It simply keeps the individual in the group which is the recipient of God's grace' (p. 420). The question was then asked, if the Judaism of the day was not legalistic, do we not have to think again what Paul really meant when he contrasted justification by faith and by works?

Alongside this radical challenge Saunders introduced a set of other proposals which also tended to undermine traditional readings of Paul. He suggested that the direction of Paul's soteriology was not, as one might have expected, from human predicament to its solution in Christ. Paul began rather with Christ as the solution and from there deduced that the human plight was simply to be without Christ. Further, Saunders argued that 'participatory' categories, that is, the range of concepts which are related to 'being in Christ', are more dominant in Pauline thought than those that are derived from the law courts, such as justification and pardon.

> There should, however, be no doubt as to where the heart of Paul's theology lies. He is not primarily concerned with juristic categories, although he works with them. The real bite of his theology lies in the participatory categories, even though *he himself did not distinguish them this way.* (p. 502)

Scholars like James Dunn, Richard Hays and N. T. Wright have sought in their various ways to develop the implications of the work of Saunders for our reading of Paul, radically reworking traditional interpretations in the process.

In this chapter we will confine our study to Tom Wright's reassessment of Paul's thought, not because he is the 'leader' of this somewhat diverse movement, but because he is the most widely read of its writers and offers, in my view, the most comprehensive and systematic alternative to that of the tradition.

HISTORY, COVENANT AND APOCALYPSE

Wright has all the instincts of a born historian. His mammoth studies on Christian origins give indication of a mind that is able to inhabit the historical world he is studying with a remarkable sensitivity to the issues and questions that form it. He is particularly aware that a person's ideas are shaped by their context and need to be interpreted in the light of it. When considering the Pauline corpus he is ever ready to think through what it meant to be a Jew moulded by the religious aspirations and hopes of Second Temple Judaism, but who also inhabited a world dominated by Greek culture and lived as a free citizen of the Roman Empire. Wright's emphasis on the significance of history for our understanding of the text means that he tends to privilege theological meaning that is discovered in the unfolding historical process over that which is derived from abstract or ahistorical concepts.

Alongside his doctoral studies on Romans and his later publication of a major commentary on the epistle, Wright also brings to the study of Paul a background of research into the notion of covenant, believing it to be a key hermeneutic tool in reading Paul correctly. Another dimension of Wright's theological interests reflected in his approach to Paul's thought has to do with eschatology. Wright is deeply committed to the ongoing integrity of creation believing that at the end the earth and all creation with it will not be abandoned but renewed by God. Earth will not finally be destroyed, rather, it will be remade. Heaven and earth should not, according to him, be conceived of dualistically. They will at the end be brought together.

Although Wright has written extensively on matters that relate to Paul's doctrine of justification, he has fortunately brought most of his key ideas together in one short and easy-to-read book, *What St Paul Really Said*. I will use this as the basic text of this study, but will also draw on other material as required.

CRITIQUE OF THE TRADITION

There are two features of the basic scheme of justification employed by the Western Church these past 1,500 years which Wright strongly opposes – its non-historical nature and its focus on personal salvation. Let us look more closely what he means by these notions and consider why he is so against them. First, what is implied by a non-historical view of salvation?

[F]or many Christians within the Protestant traditions the ideas of continuing history as having importance in itself, and of expecting deliverance within history is not on the radar screen . . . they shake their heads and settle back into the comfort of a non-historical soteriology and the short of which is 'my relationship with God' rather than 'what God is going to do to sort out his world and his people. (*Justification*, pp. 42, 43)[3]

What is the theological practice underlying the position that Wright is opposing? It is, as I understand it, the view that God might deal with humankind in a way that is not historically conditioned, that he acts among us according to principles which we could call time-less. For instance, traditional dogmatics holds that the grounds and terms on which God promises to be gracious to Abraham and pledges to be his God are applicable to all the children of promise of all ages and cultures irrespective of their particular historical circumstances. Although the outward administration of God's cov-enant with Abraham might be altered, its promises are in essence the promises of the gospel and they remain basically unqualified by time or place. Now the notion described above that God's promise of salvation in Christ to the wider world is in its essential elements independent of time, place or situation is anathema to Wright's his-torical sensibilities.

The second concern that Wright has with the traditional Western model of salvation is its inherent self-centredness. '*We* are in orbit around *God and his purposes*, not the other way around. If the Reformation tradition had treated the Gospels as equally impor-tant to the epistles, this mistake might never have happened' (*Justification*, p. 8). This is a somewhat odd statement to make given the fact that Calvin's theology is generally characterized by his determination to give glory only to God. Nevertheless, there is throughout Wright's writing a deep conviction that the individual's interest in his or her own personal salvation is somehow inappropri-ate. Why is this? What is the theological issue at stake that Wright believes he must oppose? It appears to me that Wright is deeply concerned with a modern form of Pietism, which can be described, at least in part, as that focus on human piety that fails to take full account of God's wider mission to the world and fails to participate fully in it. But further than that Wright disapproves of an emphasis on personal salvation and particularly the notion that humans play some part in the gospel dynamic of divine promise and responsive faith. If humans have something to do in the appropriation of salva-tion then, argues Wright, it becomes all about them and the aware-ness of God's greater purpose in the world and creation is in danger of being lost. This concern helps us to understand why he will not concede that faith is instrumental in salvation.

'Faith', for Paul, is therefore not a substitute 'work' in a moral-istic sense. It is not something one does in order to gain admit-tance in the covenant people. It is the badge that proclaims that one is already a member. (*What St Paul Really Said*, p. 132)

Knowing something of Wright's theological concerns can be a help in understanding why he argues as he does. It does not, of course, resolve the issue of whether or not his arguments are correct. These need to be assessed on their own merits, for the factors which shape or motivate a person's opinion have no bearing on the legitimacy of those opinions. But they are a guide to why he chooses, as we shall see, to shun the old pathways and ventures out on an almost unused track to explain what God has done for the salvation of the world.

There are two components in Wright's project. On the one hand he presents an alternative narrative of salvation to that of the Western tradition. On the other he seeks to show that Western theologians have for the greater part of their history radically misunderstood what Paul means by justification. Let us consider first his positive proposal regarding the story of salvation.

A NARRATIVE OF SALVATION

Wright understands Paul's theology to be shaped by an understanding of 'the story of Israel, and of the whole world, as a single continuous narrative which, having reached its climax in Jesus the Messiah, was now developing in the fresh ways which God the creator, the Lord of history, had always intended' (*Justification*, p. 17). What is the outline of this salvation narrative?

God's one plan is to bless the world, or put it to rights, through his people Israel. This plan is revealed in the covenant that he made with Abraham outlined in Genesis 15 and in the great covenantal promises and warnings given in Deuteronomy 27–30.[4] Israel, however, has throughout its history proved to be faithless, failing to fulfil its commission to 'be a blessing to the world. What is required if the world's sin is to be dealt with and a new creation established is a faithful Israelite who will fulfil the salvation purposes of the covenant. Jesus, the Messiah of Jewish expectation is that faithful person. In him the promised hope of a true return from exile will be fulfilled, the divine lordship over all creation effected and the world put to rights. 'The cross is for Paul the symbol, as it was the means, of the liberating victory of the one true God, the creator of the world, over all the enslaving powers that have usurped his authority' (*What St Paul Really Said*, p. 47). Through the cross evil has been defeated at its heart so that God's justice and order may be restored to the cosmos.

The resurrection is the demonstration of the lordship of the risen Jesus over the whole world, its rulers and its powers. The gospel is the proclamation of that lordship, it is the divine summons of obedience to Jesus as king and renunciation of other loyalties. 'But if the heralding of this gospel was the authoritative summons to allegiance, it could not but pose a challenge to all other "powers" that claimed human loyalty' (*What St Paul Really Said*, p. 61). The Spirit works in the lives of those who hear this announcement and they come to believe the message. Faith is not an instrument through which salvation is attained but rather a marker of the true people of God.

The set of ideas, outlined here, in Wright's narrative of salvation are all closely related. Together they form what we might call an interpretative theory, a way of making sense of the otherwise bewildering assortment of notions and themes that comprise the Pauline corpus. Wright's 'explanatory theory' is put forward as an alternative to other theories or hermeneutical schemes, most notably to the doctrine of justification as it has been broadly expounded in the Western Church.

JUSTIFYING THE SALVATION-THROUGH-ISRAEL MODEL

The heart of Wright's interpretative scheme is God's single plan to reorder the world through Israel and this plan is in essence his covenant with Abraham. Wright's first task is to show that Paul had such a view of the covenant and that this view determined his theology.

The problem before Wright is that although Paul does hold that God will bless the world through Abraham and his seed, he emphasizes that the seed is but one person – Jesus Christ (Gal. 3.16). Paul never goes on to say that God's purpose is to save the world through Israel. Wright acknowledges that the direct references in the Pauline corpus to the covenant, operating in this way, are limited, but holds that there are a number of allusions to the concept which, when read carefully, indicate that the narrative story suggested in his reading of the covenant with Abraham does in fact shape Paul's theology.

> [W]hen we look at the evidence for the single plan-of-the-creator-through-Abraham-and-Israel-for the world we discover tell-tale indications of how Paul might have spoken further. (*Justification*, p. 76)

Wright is only able to claim that his theory is hinted at in the text, that Paul might have supported it if he had spoken further. The second notion that he needs to demonstrate as having a formative role in Paul's theology is that of Jesus as the faithful Israelite. Jesus is the one who accomplishes what Israel itself failed to do. Wright uses two arguments to achieve this. First, he maintains that when Paul uses the word 'Christ' he is referring to Jesus' identity as the royal Messiah of Jewish expectation and that the expression 'Jesus Christ' when employed by Paul might be better translated 'Jesus is the Messiah'. Secondly, he holds that the Greek expression *pistos christou* usually understood as 'faith in Christ' should actually be rendered as the 'faithfulness of Christ'. Taken together these arguments indicate that Paul did have an understanding of Jesus as the faithful Israelite. Wright's difficulty is that both of these readings are widely challenged by scholars including those from within his own circle. Even if we were to allow these arguments, they would only show that the Pauline texts 'hint at' the idea that Jesus is the faithful Israelite. Contrast this with the notion that Jesus is the second Adam. Paul repeatedly makes this identification explicit and uses it to establish important theological conclusions (see Rom. 5.12-19; 1 Cor. 15.20-22). If the idea that Jesus is the faithful Israelite does in fact lie at the very centre of Paul's exposition of salvation and is to be used as a hermeneutic tool, one would expect to see it spelled out more clearly in the text.

The third feature of Wright's theory of salvation is that the gospel is the announcement of the lordship of Jesus. As the royal Messiah, he has triumphed over the forces of evil in the cross, a victory which was demonstrated by his defeat of death in the resurrection. This interpretation of Christ's death is proposed by Wright as preferential to the traditional Western theory that Jesus' atoning work was priestly, sacrificial and centred on ideas such as justification and reconciliation. How strong is the textual support for this notion that the gospel is the announcement of the lordship of Christ? Wright argues from Isaiah 40 that the good news has to do with the coming of God as the rightful king of Israel. This he says is much how the word *euaggelion* was used in the Roman world to describe the accession of an emperor. But we might ask: 'What about Paul? When he spoke of the gospel did he simply mean the lordship of Christ?' Wright maintained that he did and finds support for his theory in the first chapter of Romans. '[T]he gospel he promised beforehand through his prophets in the Holy Scriptures regarding his Son, who as to his human nature was a descendant of David, and who through the Spirit of holiness was declared with power to be the Son of God by his resurrection from the dead: Jesus Christ our Lord (Rom. 1.2-4). The gospel, according to Wright, is about Jesus being declared to be the Lord through his resurrection from the dead. Such an interpretation of these verses goes against the almost universal consensus of Pauline scholarship which has considered this passage to be Christological rather than soteriological. Wright explains why he takes an independent line.

> Generations of scholars, determined to resist the idea that Paul thought of Jesus in any way as the king, the Messiah, the true Son of David, have of course allowed this passage to drop off the front of Romans, as they hurried on to what they took to be the real introductory formula in verses 16-17, the announcement of the righteousness of God. (*What St Paul Really Said*, pp. 52, 53)

In each of the three areas outlined above Wright is well aware that it can be charged against him that he is imposing his salvation narrative of 'God's one plan to put the world to rights through Israel' onto the text rather than discovering it in the text, in short, that his project has more to do with eisogesis than exegesis. But, confronted with such a charge Wright argues that finding even a hint of the concept or the story in the text is quite enough.

> When we find allusions to the same stories (from Jewish literature) in Paul we are not merely invited but obliged to take them up and lay bare the narrative world he would have taken for granted. Within second-Temple Judaism, we must resist the cautious minimalism that threatens here as elsewhere to reduce scholarship to embattled silence. (*Paul: Fresh Perspectives*, p. 8)[5]

SALVATION TYPES

One of the interesting features in the comparative study of religions is the attempt to characterize the nature or type of various religious communities. For instance, Saunders categorizes Second

Temple Judaism as 'covenantal nomism'. Whether this term happens to be appropriate or not, the analysis of the way a religion functions appears to be brimful of illuminating insights. How might we categorize the type of religion outlined above in Wright's narrative of salvation? Let us first remind ourselves of its determining features.

The human predicament is conceived of as our subjection to the powers of evil and disorder, rather than in terms of our sin, accountability and subjection to divine judgement. God's purpose for the world is consequently understood as the restoration of good governance. 'The covenant was there to put the world to rights, to deal with evil and to restore God's justice and order to the cosmos' (*What St Paul Really Said*, p. 117). Christ's messianic role is royal and not priestly and his cross is understood primarily as the defeat of evil rather than as atonement for sin.

> The cross is for Paul the symbol, as it was the means, of the liberating victory of the one true God, the creator of the world, over all the enslaving powers that have usurped his authority . . . Instead of a great military victory over Rome, Jesus as the representative Israelite had won a great victory over sin and death, the real enemies of the people of God and of the whole world. (*What St Paul Really Said*, pp. 47, 93)

The gospel is interpreted as the lordship of Christ in preference to the notion that he died for our sins. The form of the gospel is that of a divine summons rather than a promise of grace. Its hearers are called to obedience rather than to faith.

> The royal proclamation is not simply the conveying of true information about the kingship of Jesus. It is the putting into effect of that kingship, the decisive and authoritative summoning to allegiance. Paul discovered, at the heart of his missionary practice, that when he announced the lordship of Jesus Christ, the sovereignty of King Jesus, this very announcement was the means by which the living God reached out with his love and changed the hearts of men and women. (*What St Paul Really Said*, p. 61)

What of the concept of pardon? Wright does on occasion refer to it, but he does so only in passing. It does not function as an integral feature of his scheme. He does not describe a predicament which would require it or discuss the consequences that result from it. One could say that he uses it in much the same way that I would as a young Protestant in a Catholic school cross myself when saying public prayers. I did it in deference to those around me but it had no abiding place in my theological make-up.

How are we to characterize the sort of religion suggested here? I quote from my earlier study on the atonement.

> [Wright's] structure is attractively simple. Shaped by a small, integrated set of ideas relating to governance, including those of authority, power, victory, order, allegiance and obedience it is able to avoid a number of classical theological dilemmas that a soteriology might have which is ordered by a broader range of concepts. Wright's somewhat militaristic matrix of controlling ideas provides an alternative interpretative scheme, a particular way of approaching the biblical material about salvation, one which is shaped by questions of governance. In so doing, it replaces a hermeneutical scheme that has tended to focus mainly on relationships – how they are constituted, broken and restored. (*Promise of Peace*, p. 111)[6]

In terms of the way it functions I suggest that the controlling motif of Wright's soteriology is 'the reinstatement of good governance through the kingship of Jesus' or, in the evocative jargon of the comparative study of religions, 'messianic nomism'. If one removed from his exposition of justification the few passing references to relational concepts such as grace, mercy, pardon and reconciliation, the structure would stand intact. None of these concepts serve as load-bearing beams. They are, however, integral features of Paul's soteriology. This means that if my outline above provides even a moderately fair summary of Wright's narrative of salvation, then that narrative is alien to the Pauline text and cannot serve as a successful interpretative tool for his theology.

Wright's failure to provide a model of salvation that faithfully reflects Paul's thought does not mean that he is unsuccessful in the second aspect of his project, that is, his critique of the traditional Western understanding of justification and his provision of an alternative interpretation of it. And it is to the consideration of these that we now turn.

JUSTIFICATION IN WESTERN THOUGHT

Wright, along with his colleagues, seeks to offer a viable alternative to the traditional Western doctrine of justification, which he believes has radically misread Paul's use of the concept ever since Augustine. Part of the reason, he suggests, for this misunderstanding is that the doctrine of justification has been continuously employed by its expositors for polemical purposes.

> Classically, this doctrine ever since Augustine has been concerned with warding off some version or other of the Pelagian heresy. (*What St Paul Really Said*, p. 116)

If we are to properly assess Wright's critique of the Western doctrine of justification, we need to go beyond caricature and remind ourselves of what that doctrine actually is.

In Western thought justification is, in essence, the divine act of pardon, founded on the atoning death of Christ, whereby the ungodly are made to be righteous. For Augustine this new righteousness includes transformation of life; Aquinas expounded it in terms of right relationships; Luther emphasized the imputation of Christ's righteousness. But dominating all their accounts is the idea of divine forgiveness. Justification is, at its heart, the saving act of divine pardon which establishes peace between God and the sinner. Through it men and women are reconciled to him.

The Western church has uniformly held that justification is received through the exercise of human faith, where faith is conceived in terms of both intellectual conviction and responsive trust. The Pelagian controversy was a debate about whether it was possible for human faith to respond to God apart from divine grace, while the Catholic–Protestant dispute centred on the question of whether it was faith *alone* that justified. The issues, as we have seen, were complex and the arguments detailed. All parties, however, agreed on the necessity of faith in salvation.

The principal teachers of the Western Church up to and including those of the Reformation have also held consistently that the righteousness of God is the righteousness which God brings about in the ungodly. It is the justifying judgement of God. It flows from his character and reflects the righteousness of his person, but it is not itself a divine attribute or characteristic. In technical terms we might say that the 'righteousness of God' is a genitive of origin – the righteousness that comes from God; this sometimes overlaps with a conception of it as a subjective genitive – the justifying act of God. It was not, however, considered to be a possessive genitive – God's personal righteousness.

This brief schematization of the Western doctrine of justification is a way of bringing its representatives, including the much parodied Pelagius, into the proverbial seminar room in order that, when in the next section Wright presents his own interpretation of what Paul means by justification, they might help to balance the discussion.

A NEW PERSPECTIVE

The heart of Wright's argument is that the Western Church has been wrong to interpret justification as an aspect of salvation. 'Paul may or may not agree with Augustine, Luther or anyone else about how people come to a personal knowledge of God in Christ; but he does not use the language of "justification" to denote this event or process' (*What St Paul Really Said*, p. 117). When Paul does use speak of justification he is, maintains Wright, talking about the church. He summarizes his position succinctly.

> For Paul, 'the gospel' creates the church; justification defines it. (*What St Paul Really Said*, p. 151)

The significance of such a claim is not to be underestimated. If the doctrine of justification is not actually about salvation, some 1,500 years of Western Christian scholarship on the subject have completely missed the point. Such things do happen. A long and universally held consensus can be quite wrong. Remember what happened to the Aristotelian cosmology! Nevertheless, when Wright presents his case we would be wise to bear in mind the enormity of the claim he is making.

It is Wright's argument that justification has to do with defining the people of God. The Jews understood themselves to be demarcated as a people in covenant with God by their fulfilment of the demands of the Torah, by the works of the law. But Paul taught the newly formed Christian churches that all who believe the gospel of Jesus Christ, both Jews and Gentiles, 'are demarcated by their faith – specifically by their believing of the "gospel" message of the sovereignty of Jesus Christ' (*What St Paul Really Said*, p. 132). It is faith not works that marks them off as the people of God.

This doctrine of justification is, Wright holds, pastoral in intent. Through it Paul is seeking to give assurance to those who might doubt that they are included in the community of God. If they recognize in themselves the marks of a new faith in the gospel of Jesus then they can be sure they do indeed belong. '[J]ustification was not the message he would announce on the street of the puzzled pagans of (say) Corinth; it was not the main thrust of his evangelistic message. It was the things his converts most needed to know in order to be assured that they really were part of God's people' (*What St Paul Really Said*, p. 94). This strategy for giving assurance is not dissimilar to the way seventeenth-century Puritan pastors might have encouraged anxious members of their congregations to look to certain features of their own spirituality or behavioural patterns as indicators that they were indeed to be numbered among the elect. So it is that the doctrine of justification is understood by Wright, neither as an aspect of God's saving work nor as lying at the heart of the gospel message, but as a theology of assurance.

> 'Justification' is then the doctrine which declares that whoever believes that gospel, and wherever and whenever they believe it, those people are truly members of his family. (*What St Paul Really Said*, p. 151)

Both the content and the structure of the above statement appear remarkably similar to what we might find in a classical exposition of justification. But a subtle shift or transposition has taken place in the final phrase. Instead of talking about salvation we find ourselves using much the same language as before to say something about membership in the church. How did this change take place? An assumed distinction has been introduced into the argument without us being quite aware of what was happening. It is a distinction between the experience of salvation and membership of the church, between soteriology and ecclesiology. But in this context there can be no such neat differentiation. To be a child of Abraham means both to belong to a particular community and to participate in eternal salvation. The one cannot be divorced from the other. It is a mistake to suggest that justification refers to church membership and not to salvation. For Paul, being a child of Abraham means inheriting all the promises of eternal salvation: 'it is the children of the promise who are regarded as Abraham's offspring' (Rom. 9.8b).

Being encouraged to focus on the distinction, improper in this context, between salvation and church membership, we can easily overlook the matter which is in fact pivotal to the whole argument. It has to do with the role of faith. Wright holds that faith is a marker of membership among the people of God. However, the real issue is whether faith is *no more than* a marker of those who are to receive eternal life. Is faith not instrumental in their salvation? For Wright's thesis to hold, faith cannot play any role in the event of salvation. For if the promises of the gospel and the covenant are appropriated by faith, then the 'marker' role of faith is secondary and pastorally irrelevant. The anxious pilgrim needs to be encouraged to look not to his or her wavering faith for confidence, but rather to the promises of God in Christ, to the sufficiency of Jesus' life and death. Focusing on one's own uncertain faith is always destructive of that faith, the proper nature of which is to look away from itself and towards the graciousness of God.

The issue at stake in the 'faith is merely a marker theory' is whether Paul did or did not view faith as instrumental in salvation. Wright consistently denies that he did. Consider his exposition of the passage in Philippians where Paul speaks of his personal desire to have 'the righteousness that comes from God and is by faith' (Phil. 3.9b).

> Is faith something I 'do' to earn God's favour, and, if not, what role does it play? Once we release Paul's justification language from the burden of having to describe 'how someone becomes a Christian', however, this is simply no longer a problem. There is no danger of imagining that Christian faith is after all a surrogate 'work', let alone a substitute form of moral righteousness. (*What St Paul Really Said*, p. 125)

The Church has long battled to explain the place of saving or justifying faith in such a way as not to compromise the sovereignty and graciousness of God in salvation. This is what the Pelagian controversy was all about. What has not been attempted, until very recently, is to exclude the role of faith in salvation in order to resolve the complex relation between divine and human agency. But faith cannot be expunged from the saving dynamic in this way. There is hardly a more fundamental or foundational notion in the New Testament than that of the instrumental role of faith in salvation. Paul suggests that those who fail to recognize it have come under a magician's spell.

> You foolish Galatians! Who has bewitched you? Before your very eyes Jesus Christ was clearly portrayed as crucified. I would like to learn just one thing from you. Did you receive the Spirit by observing the law, or by believing what you have heard? Are you so foolish? (Gal. 3.1-3a)

It is the consistent witness of the epistles and the Gospels that salvation is appropriated through faith in God and trust in his promises. A theological scheme which fails to acknowledge this is at odds with very heart of the biblical testimony.

CONCLUSION

Two days before his death Luther wrote on a note of paper.

> No one can understand Virgil in his Bucolics and Georgics until he has been a shepherd or a farmer for fifty years. No one can understand Cicero in his letters unless he has been involved for twenty years in the life of a powerful state. Let no one think he has tasted Holy Scripture unless he has for a century *ecclesias gubernarit* and has been responsible for the Church.[7]

What sort of background or experience is necessary to grasp the thought of Paul? I suggest that one needs the heart and passion of an evangelist. One must be able to share in some measure in the 'great sorrow and unceasing anguish' that he has for his fellow countrymen and appreciate why it is that he is willing to forfeit his life for their salvation? The interpreter who has no empathy with his stated aim to become 'all things to all people so that by all possible means I might save some' is unlikely to recognize the dynamic that drives his theology of salvation. According to Luke, even kings were subjected to his irrepressible evangelistic fervour:

> Then Agrippa said to Paul, 'Do you think that in such a short time you can persuade me to be a Christian?' Paul replied,

'Short time or long – I pray God that not only you but all who are listening to me today may become what I am, except for these chains.' (Acts 26.28, 29)

The expositor who is embarrassed by this passionate concern for an individual's personal salvation is unlikely to do justice to Paul. The gospel lies at the centre of all his thinking. It defines his calling and determines his ministry. He will proclaim it at every opportunity. He will defend it with all his intellectual skills. He is ruthless in opposing those who would alter it. He has been imprisoned for it and is ready, if need be, to die for it.

The whole structure of Wright's exposition suggests to me that he has not identified with Paul in the matter that most determines his ministry, his calling as an evangelist. From start to finish Paul's consuming interest is in the gospel 'as the power of God that brings salvation to everyone who believes'. He strives for the reconciliation of communities to God and so to one another and he seeks the salvation of the individuals that comprise them. The discussion in his letter to the Romans about who are the true Jews and what is the future of Israel is a defence of the unchangeable nature of God's gospel promises in the covenant. The inclusion of the Gentiles into Abraham's family is the immediate implication of the same gospel. The discourse on sanctification and the renewal of creation is the outworking of the message of the gospel. The epistle to the Romans is not an academic paper on the relationship between Christians and Jews which is to be presented to the university's Comparative Study of Religions' seminar. It is rather the work of a remarkable, clear sighted and passionate evangelist plying his trade. And it all has to do with the gospel.

In summary, it seems to me that Wright has imposed an alien narrative of salvation on the Pauline text, a narrative whose structure is governmental rather than relational and is concerned more with right order than it is with grace. He has been satisfied with misleading parodies of both the Pelagian debate and the Catholic Church's presentation of salvation in its dispute with Luther. This has contributed to his failure to recognize how a classical Western interpretation of justification is applicable both to the Judaism of Paul's day and the human condition in general. In his own exposition of justification he has relied on a false distinction between membership of the family of Abraham and reconciliation with God and has never shown, as his theory requires, how the Pauline text requires that faith is not instrumental in salvation. He has assumed, wrongly in my estimation, that his own aversion to timeless theological concepts is a perspective that is shared by Paul. Finally, I believe he has failed to take proper account of the determining characteristic of Paul's ministry, that is, his role as an evangelist, with a passion to preach, protect, expound and develop the implications of the gospel.

Wright's work is part of a larger project, loosely described as the New Perspective. It is a bold and imaginative attempt to give fresh currency to the concept of justification in a context where the notions of guilt, alienation and judgement no longer shape our understanding of the human predicament. In seeking to do this it has construed justification in terms of church membership. I have argued above that such a programme fails for all sort of reasons, not least of which is the fact that in Paul's thought justification *is* about salvation, it has to do with the gospel.

What is the gospel of which Paul is not ashamed? It is directly related to a concept he describes as the 'righteousness of God'. Drawing on the resources of Western thought, I will in the final chapter seek to describe the nature of that righteousness and its relationship to the notion of accountability as it is experienced today.

CHAPTER 10

JUSTIFICATION TODAY

I have argued that the doctrine of justification is dependent on an understanding of the human predicament in terms of sin, guilt and judgement. We could say that they are related to one another as a medicine is to the disease for which it serves as a cure. Their close association means that anyone trying to explain the meaning of justification must have one eye on the plight for which this saving act offers a solution. Attention to this relation has shaped both the structure of this book and the analysis of the soteriology of each of the theologians we have considered. When a view of the human predicament in terms of estrangement and accountability is no longer persuasive, a doctrine of justification is bound to fall into disuse, for it no longer resolves a felt religious need in the community. In the seventh and eight chapters I have outlined some of the factors that have led to such a change in the perception of the human plight in more modern times. In the ninth chapter I highlighted the difficulties that face New Testament scholars today who would seek to explain the concept of justification apart from its intimate connexion to the notions of accountability and divine judgement. I have, of course, made an assumption that we now live in an age in which these ideas are not significant aspects of the Christian religious consciousness. Such an assumption, however, is not entirely correct.

A NEW AWARENESS OF HUMAN ACCOUNTABILITY AND GUILT

The theologians of liberation were among the first to challenge the prevailing consensus that God never has occasion to be really displeased with us. After Vatican II they began to question the unfair and dehumanizing social structures that had come to pervade so much of South American life and recognized that the Church was often deeply complicit in them. The Jesuit, Jon Sobrino, was one of those who argued persuasively that the Christ of the Gospels demands a commitment to the cause of those who are being treated unjustly.

> Considering Christ as Love, for example, Christians maintain an apparent neutrality vis-à-vis the flagrant inequalities in our society. Such neutrality is wholly contrary to the partiality that Jesus displayed in favour of the oppressed.[1]

Using what has become known as a hermeneutic of suspicion he held that those who stand to benefit from a grossly unfair and unequally structured society will naturally want to present Christ as universally loving, and manipulate the doctrine of God so that he remains aloof from the pains of our world and is not deeply offended by its injustice. But the biblical witness presents a quite different view of Jesus:

> He proclaims the coming utopia; he denounces injustice as the epitome of sin; he shows partiality towards the oppressed; he unmasks alienating religious mechanisms. And he does all this so that his Spirit will not remain vague and that his God the Father will not remain abstract and manipulable.[2]

Those who would study theology with no commitment to theological praxis, that is, to its practical application to the situations of life in an unjust world, and fail to repent of their own misuse of power, lie under divine condemnation. 'The real sinners are the persons with power who use it both to secure themselves against God and to oppress others. This leads them to deny both the future ordained by God and anticipatory embodiments of his coming reign.'[3]

Following along the path opened up by the liberation theologians, proponents of black theology applied much the same hermeneutic to the racial inequalities prevalent in North America. James H. Cone, one of its most outspoken early voices, encourages us to reconsider the place of wrath in the divine nature.

Is it possible to understand what God's love means for the oppressed without making wrath an essential ingredient of that love? What could love possibly mean in a racist society except the righteous condemnation of everything racist?[4]

Cone recognizes that the distinction between the righteousness of God in the Old Testament and the love of God in the New Testament is a form of the Marcionite heresy, one which the biblical texts simply do not support. God in his righteousness opposes racism for it is inimical to Christian existence and stands under his divine judgement. 'To speak of a "racist Christian" or a "segregated church of Christ" is blasphemy and the antithesis of the Christian gospel.'[5] Cone argues that any theology with Jesus at its centre has to be ardently committed to truth and justice and must be willing to use the language of condemnation to achieve them.

Because black theology is survival theology it must speak with a passion consistent with the depths of the wounds of the oppressed. Theological language is passionate language, the language of commitment, because it is language which seeks to vindicate the afflicted and condemn the enforcers of evil.[6]

Perhaps the most far reaching and radical critique of the structures of society is that offered by Feminism. Time and again male-dominated institutions have opposed each new demand for equality that feminists have brought forward, including universal suffrage, the right to financial independence, to attend university, to hold political office and to receive an equal wage. Their programme is, however, far from over. It is apparent that across the world in both church and society men in various contexts continue to disenfranchise, exploit, oppress, degrade and abuse women. Some feminists believe that Christian institutions and theological structures are so irredeemably opposed to bringing about justice for women that the Christian faith itself is compromised. Daphne Hampson argues that: 'feminism represents the death-knell of Christianity as a viable religious option.'[7] Others like Rosemary Ruether have discovered in the life of Jesus the pattern for a more righteous way of living in this world in the context of gender discrimination:

Jesus as the Christ . . . manifests the kenosis of patriarchy, the announcement of the new humanity through a lifestyle that discards hierarchical class privilege and speaks on behalf of the lowly . . . Jesus, the homeless Jewish prophet, and the marginalised women and men who respond to him represent the overthrow of the present world system and the sign of a dawning new age in which God's will is done on earth.[8]

Far from living without guilt or a sense of accountability before God, there are many of us today who find ourselves overwhelmed by our failure to stand up for the cause of the oppressed, to defend racial minorities, to respond to the cries of the poor or to challenge structures that are manifestly unfair to one sex. New areas of structural injustice are continually being brought to our attention. We have now come to recognize that much of the imported food we eat is produced by people who are not given a fair wage and that the cheap clothes on our backs are inexpensive partly because of the exploitation of women and children in their manufacture. It would seem that the levels of luxury we take for granted are to some extent dependent on the suffering or mistreatment of those who cannot speak up or defend themselves. Further, we have come to learn in recent decades that through our apparently insatiable corporate greed we are damaging our planet, depleting its natural resources, polluting its atmosphere, destroying countless species of flora and fauna and robbing our children of their natural inheritance. The voices that speak of our culpability and judgement do not all have religious accents, but we hear them nevertheless as a form of God's Word calling us to account. They reflect a theme that is timeless.

> He has shown you, O man, what is good.
> And what does the LORD require of you?
> To act justly and to love mercy
> and to walk humbly with your God. (Mic. 6.8)

Other voices also speak to our consciences. They highlight the damage brought about by our failures as parents or partners, they scold us for our destructive addictions and reprimand us for failing to fulfil our potential. For many these disturbing words of demand and accusation come as principles of universal truth, as the precepts of a transcendent law. There is, of course, much in them that is also to be found in the sayings of the prophets, but their status as inviolable law is affirmed by many whose ideas are not informed by the Christian scriptures. Before such law, and we have here no more than a cursory introduction to its legitimate demands, all our excuses and explanations appear hollow and self-serving. The affirming strategies of our personal therapists often miss the real point. We are guilty as charged and there is nothing further to be said in our defence. As Paul argues: the law speaks to us in this way 'so that every mouth may be silenced and the whole world held accountable to God' (Rom. 3.19).

If this outline describes even in small part our modern experience of the human plight, how is the doctrine of justification to be applied to those who find themselves caught up in it? How can it be for them a solution to their sense of predicament?

A RIGHTEOUSNESS THAT COMES FROM GOD

The message of justification is a radical response to the human experience of failure, guilt and alienation in the context of our recognized obligations to our neighbours, our families, our planet and our God to live justly in this world. It is a message that appears to be highly suspect morally, particularly, among those who have given themselves to the search for a more righteous way of living in a world shot through with injustice. The doctrine, when applied to the modern predicament might take the following form.

The God, who has demanded of us that we live with loving responsibility towards our neighbours and in faithful relation to him, showing due care for his creation, has now made known a different way of being righteous, a way that is suggested by the Hebrew scriptures. It is a righteousness that it is not dependent on us fulfilling our moral and religious obligations, for it is plain that we have all tragically failed in that and will continue to do so. It is, rather, a righteousness that God brings into effect, a righteousness that is for those who wholeheartedly take hold of the person of Jesus Christ and become enveloped in his life. For it is the message of the gospel that God has lovingly given his own Son as a form of ransom payment so that we might be released from the responsibility we bear for the evil we have done to our fellows. Jesus' willing sacrificial death is an offering for our sins, an effective cry to his Father to be merciful to us and not treat us as our deeds and attitudes so clearly deserve. He has borne the divine curse or judgement against our wrongdoing. By dealing with us in this way God demonstrates his own moral righteousness. Justice, contrary to the opinion of many, has been properly served in this primal act of love, the free giving-over of his Son to death for those who are his enemies.

This divine act of making us righteous or justifying us is, at its heart, an act of pardon or forgiveness. Although we have oppressed, abused and neglected the weak or have connived in the actions of others who have done so, we are through faith in Jesus Christ now reckoned to be righteous in the sight of God. Our broken relationship with him is reconstituted. We have entered a state of peace with God.

But further than that, having being caught up in the life of Jesus we are progressively transformed by God through the power of his Spirit so that we now at last begin to live as he requires. We are liberated from our bondage to self-centredness. The principal characteristic manifest in this newly created, Spirit-empowered way of life is love. We begin to do right by our neighbours not simply because it is required of us, rather, we act justly because we want to do so. Our determination to strive for justice is motivated by love and it is expressed in a humility that befits those who have themselves failed so badly and continue to do so. We find that it is only as we become great lovers overwhelmed by the Spirit of Jesus that we start to satisfy the righteous demands of the law.

At the end, each one of us will be required to give a full account of our lives before the risen Christ, the plenipotentiary of God. He will graciously reward every loving act that he has accomplished among the faithful through his Spirit and grant to them the gift of eternal life. In short, those whom God has justified he will one day bring to glory.

For those who are shamed by their failure to do right by their neighbour, to care for this planet, to fulfil their divinely given potential and to walk humbly before God, and who desire for themselves a righteousness that comes from above, Paul gives this exhortation:

We are therefore Christ's ambassadors, as though God were making his appeal through us – we implore you on Christ's behalf: Be reconciled to God. God made him who knew no sin to be sin for us, so that in him we might become the righteousness of God . . . I tell you now is the time of God's favour, now is the day of salvation. (2 Cor. 5.20, 21; 6.2b)

The reader will be aware that this summary presentation of the doctrine of justification is no more than a compilation of various elements from the tradition of Western interpretation that we have been examining in this book. Let me highlight some of those strands.

GLEANING FROM THE TRADITION

Until the past hundred years or so all the principal exponents of the doctrine of justification in Western theology held that 'the righteousness of God', in the context of justification, was broadly synonymous with the expression 'the salvation of God'. It referred to the state that God brought about in the believer through his justifying act of judgement.

That such a judgement was at its heart an act of pardon was also a common element in the soteriology of the writers we have studied. Some, however, held that it entailed more than forgiveness. Augustine did not distinguish the justification of the sinner from the transformation that is an essential feature of the life of the one who is justified. Martin Luther held that other than the putting aside of our sins there is in justification a positive transference to the believer of the righteousness of Christ. It was Thomas Aquinas and John Calvin who were most clear that justification was simply divine pardon. There is great hermeneutic power in the simplicity of that interpretation: 'To justify, therefore, is nothing else than to acquit from the charge of guilt, as if innocence were proved' (*Institutes*, 3.11.3, p. 39).

It is to Luther that we owe the insight that there is in Paul's thought two quite distinct types of righteousness – a passive or alien righteousness that comes from without the believer, and an active or personal righteousness that God graciously brings about in his or her life. Justification has to do with the former and not the latter. It was also Luther who emphasized that faith was a 'taking hold' of Christ and he was bold enough to use the concept of marriage to express it. Faith meant for him embracing Jesus' person and thereby sharing in all of his riches even as he chose to share in our poverty. Calvin developed this insight and argued that 'being in Christ' was the foundational soteriological idea from which both justification and sanctification flowed. It was union with Christ that established the indissoluble link between the two, without confusing the one with the other. On the one hand, we are justified only as we are embedded in Christ. On the other, it is by being baptized into Christ's death and sharing in his resurrection life that we come to experience a new way of holiness. According to Calvin no saving benefit is experienced by us apart from our personal union with Christ.

Karl Barth appears to me to have seen most clearly that the justifying act of God in which Jesus Christ is judged in our stead is a morally righteous event that flows from God's eternally righteous nature. His action is just because he in his own person is just, and the justice of the cross is the criterion by which we are to measure all other instances of just action.

That the new life of the justified person is characterized by love or charity is a theme brilliantly highlighted in the theology of Augustine:

> See what we are insisting upon; that the deeds of men are only discerned by the root of charity. For many things may be done that have a good appearance, and yet proceed not from the root of charity. For thorns also have flowers: some actions truly seem rough, seem savage; howbeit they are done for discipline at the bidding of charity. Once for all, then, a short precept is given thee: Love, and do what thou wilt: whether thou hold thy peace, through love hold thy peace; whether thou cry out, through love cry out; whether thou correct, through love correct; whether thou spare, through love do thou spare: let the root of love be within, of this root can nothing spring but what is good. (*Seventh Homily on 1 John*)

It is on this principle of love determining our actions that we will be granted eternal life.

It was Thomas who made clear the important distinction between the justification of the ungodly and the glorification of the just. He held that justification was freely given apart from any merit on our part, while glorification was the reward granted to the righteous for what they have done in this life. Further, he argued that the determinative human characteristic in justification is that of faith, while the gracious habit which makes an action meritorious is love. I do not think that Luther fully recognized this distinction. Calvin did and was careful to explain that although works of love were necessary for the gift of eternal life, they were not the basis of it. The foundation of the gift of life eternal is the death of Christ appropriated through faith.

The summary statement of justification put forward above as a response to a modern experience of sin, guilt and alienation is no more than a consolidation of what this study has indicated to be the most secure aspects of the tradition's interpretation of the meaning of Paul. But how fair is such a summary to the Pauline text?

PAUL'S DOCTRINE OF JUSTIFICATION

The title of this subsection is misleading if it is taken to suggest that we are now embarking on a wholly different exercise from that which has engaged us in the earlier chapters. The purpose of our discussion with leading Christians in the Western tradition was precisely this, to try and determine what Paul means by justification. They all immersed themselves in the scriptures and sought in their various ways to articulate his position. I am not here attempting to put forward something different from the summary statement of justification outlined above. I am simply trying to show how it 'fits well' with some key texts in the same way as any good theory must make sense of the material before it. In this process I am, in effect, offering a defence of this particular outline of Paul's doctrine in the face of alternative interpretative schemes. Let us then briefly consider the text.

First, Paul argues that we are faced with two alternative and competing forms of righteousness – our own self-righteousness based on the law and a righteousness that is not from ourselves but comes from God and is received through faith. Sometimes he makes this distinction explicit:

[T]hat I may gain Christ and be found in him, not having a righteousness of my own that comes from the law, but that which is through faith in Christ – the righteousness that comes from God and is by faith. (Phil. 3.8b, 9)

[T]he Gentiles, who did not pursue righteousness, have obtained it, a righteousness that is by faith; but Israel, who pursued a law

of righteousness, has not attained it . . . Since they did not know
the righteousness that comes from God and sought to establish
their own, they did not submit to God's righteousness. (Rom.
9.30b, 31; 10.3)

Sometimes this distinction is implicitly made. There is a contrast
in Paul's argument in the first three chapters of Romans between
a failed human righteousness 'there is no one righteous not even
one . . . therefore no one will be declared righteous in his sight by
observing the law' and a quite different righteousness that comes
from God 'but now a righteousness apart from the law has been
made known' (Rom. 3.10, 20a, 21a). The recognition of the differentiation between these two forms of righteousness in Paul is, I
believe, the key to interpreting his doctrine of justification.

Second, and following on from the first point, *dikaiosune theou*,
the righteousness of God, is in Paul simply the new righteous state
of the believer. It is not a characteristic of God. God is rather its
author. He brings about this righteousness in his justifying judgement. 'This righteousness from God comes through faith in Jesus
Christ to all who believe' (Rom. 3.22). Against such a position it is
argued that 'the righteousness of God' is an expression that was
used by Paul in a way which was not totally new, otherwise he
would have had to explain it more clearly. This seems to me to be a
fair point. We need then to show that the phrase the 'righteousness
of God' was used to by others to refer to the righteous state of the
believer.

It is of interest that certain soteriological terms can be used
almost interchangeably in the English language. Consider these
expressions: the doctrine of atonement, the doctrine of redemption
and the doctrine of reconciliation. Although each of them when
'unpacked' refers to a somewhat different soteriological theme,
they are often used interchangeably without any specific reference to their particular meaning. For instance, we might say that
Gustaf Aulén's doctrine of atonement emphasized the role of Christ
as victor over the power of evil. Etymologically atonement has to
do with reconciliation rather than victory. Historically, it refers
to a particular day when specified sacrifices were offered by the
Jewish community. But the word atonement is generally used far
more broadly than its etymology or history might indicate. A doctrine of atonement simply means a doctrine of salvation in much

modern day theological usage. I am suggesting that the expression the 'righteousness of God' is employed repeatedly in the context which informs Paul's thought as an almost interchangeable synonym for the 'salvation of God'. There are many instances of these two phrases being used together in various forms of Hebrew parallelism. Here are some of them:

> The LORD has made his *salvation* known and revealed his *righteousness* to the nations. (Ps. 98.2)
>
> Let the earth open wide, let *salvation* spring up, let *righteousness* grow with it . . . (Isa. 45.8b)
>
> My *righteousness* draws near speedily, *my salvation* is on the way. (Isa. 51.5)
>
> But my *righteousness* will last forever, my *salvation* through all generations. (Isa. 51.8)
>
> [F]or my *salvation* is close at hand and my *righteousness* will soon be revealed. (Isa. 56.1b)
>
> He put on *righteousness* as his breastplate and the helmet of *salvation* on his head. (Isa. 59.17a)
>
> For he has clothed me with garments of *salvation* and arrayed me in a robe of *righteousness*. (Isa. 61.10b)

When Paul says that the 'righteousness of God has been made known', he is employing a well known soteriological expression from the Psalms and from Isaiah and is referring to the fulfilment of the Jewish hope for the coming salvation of God.

In similar fashion, the 'righteous acts of God' denotes, in the prophecy of Daniel, God's saving act of pardon: 'O Lord, in keeping with all your righteous acts, turn away your anger and your wrath from Jerusalem' (Dan. 9.16).

Interpreting the 'righteousness of God' as synonymous with, although not equivalent to, the 'salvation of God', sheds light on key passages in the Gospels. 'But seek first his kingdom and his righteousness, and all these things will be given to you as well' (Mt. 6.33). Jesus is referring to two overlapping concepts – salvation as the rule of God and salvation as a world of rightly ordered relationships. It would appear then that the expression the 'righteousness of God' is a widely employed soteriological term, which is broadly synonymous with the expression the 'salvation of God' but having its own particular reference, that is, to the restoration of right relationships and consequent righteous action among the faithful. Understanding the expression in this way illuminates central passages in Paul's argument. Consider how naturally the following text reads when the one set of soteriological terms is substituted by the other:

> For in the gospel the *salvation* of God is revealed, a *salvation* that is by faith from first to last, just as it is written: *'those who are saved* will live by faith.' (Rom. 1.16a, 17 altered)

The Community Rule, an illuminating document detailing the rules of a strict religious Jewish sect from the Second Temple period, employs the language of justification and the righteousness of God in ways that parallel Paul's use. We find in it that the notion of the righteousness of God in the context of human sinfulness can refer to the righteousness appropriated by the faithful with God as its author or source:

> I will declare His judgement concerning my sins and my transgressions shall be before my eyes as an engraved Precept.
>
> I will say to God, 'My Righteousness' and 'Author of my Goodness' to the Most High 'Fountain of Knowledge' and 'Source of Holiness'. (*The Community Rule* 10)[9]

Third, to justify and to pardon are broadly equivalent in the Pauline texts. 'The judgement followed one sin and brought condemnation, but the gift followed many trespasses and brought justification' (Rom. 5.16b). Justification is employed in this passage as an antonym of condemnation. Paul makes the identification of justification and pardon more explicit in his use of the idea of forgiveness in Ps. 32.1, 2 as an explanation of what it means to be accounted righteous (see Rom. 4.6-8).

Fourth, according to Paul the concepts of justification and final glorification are distinct, although related events in God's saving purposes. Believers, having being justified by faith, now have peace with God. It is their ardent hope that they will one day share in the glory of God and not come under his final condemnation. Paul encourages his readers that the God who began a saving work in them will bring it to final completion.

> Since we have now been justified by his blood, how much more shall we be saved from God's wrath through him! For if, when we were God's enemies we were reconciled to him through the death of his Son, how much more, having been reconciled, shall we be saved through his life! (Rom. 5.9, 10)

The defence of a particular doctrine of justification requires far more than the examination of a few proof texts that appear to substantiate it. Nevertheless it is important that the doctrine be seen to 'fit' the key texts naturally and also to illuminate the wider argument. And this is a judgement that every student ultimately needs to make for themselves as they engage with Paul's writings.

CONCLUSION

There is a discontinuity in the argument of this book that needs to be addressed. I have sought to show how a doctrine of justification flourished in the Western Church and in the world of thought inhabited by Paul only when there was a clear apprehension of the human predicament in terms of sin, guilt and estrangement. I have also outlined in the final chapters a movement away from this dominant world-view so that within much of the Church today the idea of Christ as the final judge of all humankind is felt to be alien and somewhat out of character with both his person and his ministry of salvation. Within this context the doctrine of justification has, as one might have expected, fallen into widespread neglect. It no longer has a place at the heart of the gospel that is proclaimed by large sections of the Western Church.

In this chapter I have traced a rather different development in the wider community with regard to the matter of accountability. It is a movement in which the demand upon us to live with integrity in a manifestly unjust world has come to challenge many aspects of our corporate and personal behaviour. A chorus of persuasive voices, external and internal, calls out for us to do better by our neighbours, our heirs and ourselves and judges us for our lapses. As to our living righteously in this world, the level of personal accountability is raised so high that many of us find ourselves overwhelmed by a sense of guilt and personal failure along with estrangement from God. Such guilt can be disempowering and destructive. It can push us to a place where we totally despair of ourselves. Now here is a strange thing. The doctrine of justification is precisely what is required as divine cure for an ailment such as this. The tragic irony is that many of the spiritual practitioners of the Western Church are now generally ill-equipped to administer such medication. No longer comfortable in affirming the radical nature of our guilt and personal accountability under a transcendent law and before a holy God, they have over the years lost the art of applying the divine remedy to those, both religious and otherwise, who have been caught up in so helpless a condition.

Perhaps the real purpose of this book is to encourage a new generation of theology students to revive that lost art.

NOTES

CHATPER 1

1 Augustine, *Confessions*, translated by R. S. Pine-Coffin (London: Penguin Books, 1977), p. 51.
2 Ibid., p. 63.
3 Ibid., p. 150.
4 Ibid., p. 43.
5 Dante, *The Divine Comedy*, translated by Dorothy L Sayers (London: Penguin Books, 1949), canto I, p. 71.
6 Canto III, p. 75.
7 Canto XX, p. 196.

CHATPER 3

1 Augustine, *The Enchiridion,* 118 *NPNF* first series, vol. 3, p. 275.
2 Ibid., p. 267.
3 See Augustine, *On the Trinity* 13.16 *NPNF* first series, vol. 3, p. 179.
4 Ibid., p. 79.
5 Augustine, *Confessions*, pp. 250–251.
6 Augustine, *The Enchiridion,* 118 *NPNF* first series, vol. 3, p. 251.
7 Ibid., p. 275.
8 Augustine, *On Man's Perfection in Righteousness*, 18, *NPNF* first series, vol. 5, p. 164.
9 Augustine, *On Nature and Grace*, 29, *NPNF* first series, vol. 5, p. 131.
10 Augustine, *On the Spirit and the Letter*, 26, *NPNF* first series, vol. 5, p. 94.
11 See Alister E. McGrath, *Justitia Dei: A History of the Christian Doctrine of Justification*, second edition (Cambridge: Cambridge University Press, 1997), p. 31.
12 Augustine, *The Enchiridion,* 118 *NPNF* first series, vol. 3, p. 259.
13 Augustine, *On the Trinity* 13.16 *NPNF* first series, vol. 3, p. 217.
14 Augustine, *On the Grace of Christ*, 1.2 *NPNF* first series, vol. 5, p. 218.
15 Augustine, *Against Julian*, 2.8.23, in 'The Fathers of the Church. A New Translation', vol. 35, p. 83.

CHATPER 4

1 Thomas Aquinas, *St Thomas Aquinas Summa Theologica*, translated by Fathers of the English Dominican Province (New York: Benziger, 1947).
2 The Pastor of Hermas, *Second Vision*, chapter 2, *ANF*, vol. 2.
3 Tertullian, *On Modesty,* chapter 21, *ANF*, vol. 4.

CHATPER 5

1 See Oliver J. Thatcher and Edgar Holmes McNeal, eds, *A Source Book for Medieval History* (New York: Scribners, 1905), pp. 513–517.
2 Martin Luther, *Ninety-Five Thesis*, in *Martin Luther: Selections from His Writings*, edited by John Dillenberger (New York: Anchor Books, 1961), p. 490.
3 Luther who chaired the disputation is recognized as having drawn up the theses.
4 Luther, *A Commentary on St Paul's Epistle to the Galatians (1531),* edited by Philip S. Watson (London: James Clarke, 1953) reprinted in *Martin Luther: Selection from His Writings,* edited by John Dillenberger (New York: Anchor Books, 1961), pp. 109, 110.
5 Quoted in Gordon Rupp, *The Righteousness of God* (London: Hodder and Stroughton, 1953), p. 114.
6 Augustine, *On the Spirit and the Letter*, 26, *NPNF* first series, vol. 5, p. 108.
7 Quoted in Gordon Rupp, *The Righteousness of God*, p. 123.
8 Luther, *Two Kinds of Righteousness*, in *Martin Luther: Selections from His Writings*, edited by John Dillenberger (New York: Anchor Books, 1961).
9 Luther, *Bondage of the Will*, in *Martin Luther: Selections from His Writings*, edited by John Dillenberger (New York: Anchor Books, 1961).
10 John Bunyan, *Grace Abounding to the Chief of Sinners*, edited by W. R. Owens (London: Penguin Books, 1987), p. 35.

CHATPER 6

1 Luther, *A Commentary on St Paul's Epistle to the Galatians (1531)*, p. 131.
2 Luther writes to Philip Melanchthon from the Wartburg in 1521: 'Be a sinner, and let your sins be strong [sin boldly], but let your trust in Christ be stronger, and rejoice in Christ who is the victor over sin, death, and the world.'
3 John Calvin, *Institutes of the Christian Religion*, translated by Henry Beveridge (Grand Rapids, MI: Eerdman's, 1970).
4 Cited by Gerhard Ebeling, *Luther*, translated by R. A. Wilson (Philadelphia: Fortress Press, 1972), pp. 123–124, noted in Mark A.

Garcia, *Life in Christ: Union with Christ and Twofold Grace in Calvin's Theology* (Milton Keynes: Pater Noster, 2008), pp. 113–114.

CHATPER 7

1 Friedrich Schleiermacher, *The Christian Faith*, edited by H. R. MacKintosh and J. S. Stewart (Edinburg: T&T Clark, 1976).
2 See Robert Merrihew Adams, 'Faith and Religious Knowledge', in *Friedrich Schleiermacher*, edited by Jacqueline Marina (Cambridge: Cambridge University Press, 2005), p. 39. Adams' analysis has been lent upon throughout this section of the chapter.
3 Ibid., p. 41.
4 H. Richard Niebuhr, *The Kingdom of God in America* (New York: Harper and Row, 1959), p. 193.

CHATPER 8

1 Karl Barth, *Protestant Theology in the Nineteenth Century*, new edition (London: SCM Press, 2001).
2 'A Thank-You and a Bow – Kierkegaard's Reveille. Speech on being awarded the Sonning Prize', in *Fragments Grave and Gay* (London: Collins, 1971), p. 97 quoted in John Webster, *Karl Barth*, second edition (London: Continuum, 2004), p. 20.
3 We arrive at the doctrine of the Trinity by no other way than that of an analysis of the concept of revelation (I.1.8.2, p. 312).
4 See *Church Dogmatics* II.2.33.1, p. 102: 'As the subject and object of this choice, Jesus Christ was at the beginning. He was not at the beginning of God, for God has indeed no beginning. But he was at the beginning of all things, at the beginning of God's dealing with the reality which is distinct from himself.'
5 Athanasius, *Four Discourses Against the Arians*, 1.5, *NPNF* second series, vol. 4, p. 309.
6 Ibid., 3.62, p. 427.
7 Ibid., 3.62, p. 427.
8 See Bruce McCormack, 'Grace and Being: The Role of God's Gracious Election in Karl Barth's Theological Ontology', in *The Cambridge Companion to Karl Barth*, edited by John Webster (Cambridge: Cambridge University Press, 2000), pp. 95–101.
9 'Qui fecit te sine te, non te justificat sine te' see *Sermones ad Populum* 169.
10 Niebuhr, *The Kingdom of God in America*, p. 193.

CHATPER 9

1 Tom Wright, *What St Paul Really Said* (Oxford: Lion Publishing, 1997), p. 113.

2   E. P. Saunders, *Paul and Palestinian Judaism* (Minneapolis: Fortress Press, 1977).
3   Tom Wright, *Justification: God's Plan and Paul's Vision* (London: SPCK, 2009).
4   Ibid., p. 75.
5   N. T. Wright, *Paul: Fresh Perspectives* (London: SPCK, 2005).
6   Alan Spence, *The Promise of Peace: A United Theory of Atonement* (London: T&T Clark, 2006).
7   Quoted from Karl Barth, *Protestant Theology in the Nineteenth Century*, p. 1.

CHATPER 10

1   Jon Sobrino, *Christianity at the Crossroads: A Latin American View* (London: SCM Press, 1978), p. xvi.
2   Ibid., p. xxv.
3   Ibid., p. 53.
4   James H. Cone, *A Black Theology of Liberation*, second edition (New York: Orbis Books, 1986), p. 69.
5   Ibid., p. 14.
6   Ibid., p. 17.
7   Daphne Hampson, *Theology and Feminism* (Oxford: Basil Blackwell, 1991), p. 1.
8   Rosemary Ruether, *Sexism and God-Talk: Towards a Feminist Theology* (Boston, MA: Beacon Press, 1983), pp. 137, 138, quoted in Hampson, *Theology and Feminism*, p. 155.
9   See G. Vermes, *The Dead Sea Scrolls in English* (London: Penguin Books, 1979), p. 90.

SELECTED BIBLIOGRAPHY

Aquinas, Thomas, *St Thomas Aquinas Summa Theologica*, translated by Fathers of the English Dominican Province (New York: Benziger, 1947).

Athanasius, *Four Discourses Against the Arians*, *NPNF*, second series, vol. 4.

Augustine, *Against Julian*, in 'The Fathers of the Church. A New Translation', vol. 35 (Washington: Catholic University of America Press, 1992).

— *Confessions*, translated by R. S. Pine-Coffin (London: Penguin Books, 1977).

— *The Enchiridion*, *NPNF* first series, vol. 3.

— *On Man's Perfection in Righteousness*, *NPNF* first series, vol. 5.

— *On Nature and Grace*, *NPNF* first series, vol. 5.

— *On the Grace of Christ*, *NPNF* first series, vol. 5.

— *On the Spirit and the Letter*, *NPNF* first series, vol. 5.

— *On the Trinity*, *NPNF* first series, vol. 3.

Barth, Karl, *Church Dogmatics*, thirteen volumes, edited by G. W. Bromily and T. F. Torrance (Edinburgh: T&T Clark, 1953–1975).

— *Protestant Theology in the Nineteenth Century* (London: SCM Press, 2001).

Brown, Peter, *Augustine of Hippo, a Biography* (London: Faber and Faber, 1967).

Bunyan, John, *Grace Abounding to the Chief of Sinners*, edited by W. R. Owens (London: Penguin Books, 1987).

Calvin, John, *Institutes of the Christian Religion*, translated by Henry Beveridge (Grand Rapids, MI: Eerdman's, 1970).

Chadwick, Henry, *Augustine of Hippo, A Life* (Oxford: Oxford University Press, 2009).

Cone, James H., *A Black Theology of Liberation*, second edition (New York: Orbis Books, 1986).

Dante, *The Divine Comedy*, translated by Dorothy L Sayers (London: Penguin Books, 1949).

Ebeling, Gerhard, *Luther*, translated by R. A. Wilson (Philadelphia: Fortress Press, 1972).

Garcia, Mark A., *Life in Christ: Union with Christ and Twofold Grace in Calvin's Theology* (Milton Keynes: Paternoster, 2008).

Hampson, Daphne, *Theology and Feminism* (Oxford: Basil Blackwell, 1991).

Luther, Martin, *Bondage of the Will*, translated by Henry Cole (Grands Rapids, MI: Baker Book House, 1979).

— *A Commentary on St Paul's Epistle to the Galatians (1531)*, edited by Philip S. Watson (London: James Clarke, 1953).

— *Ninety-Five Thesis*, in *Martin Luther: Selections from His Writings*, edited by John Dillenberger (New York: Anchor Books, 1961).

— *Two Kinds of Righteousness*, in *Martin Luther: Selections from His Writings*, edited by John Dillenberger (New York: Anchor Books, 1961).

McGrath, Alister E., *Justitia Dei: A History of the Christian Doctrine of Justification*, second edition (Cambridge: Cambridge University Press, 1997).

Mariña, Jacqueline, editor, *Friedrich Schleiermacher* (Cambridge: Cambridge University Press, 2005).

Martines, Lauro, *Scourge and Fire: Savanorola and Renaissance Italy* (London: Pimlico, 2007).

Niebuhr, H. Richard, *The Kingdom of God in America* (New York: Harper and Row, 1959).

O'Donovan, Oliver, *The Ways of Judgment* (Grands Rapids, MI: William B. Eerdmans, 2008).

The Pastor of Hermas, *Visions, ANF*, vol. 2.

Piper, John, *The Future of Justification: A Response to N. T. Wright* (Nottingham: IVP, 2008).

Ruether, Rosemary, *Sexism and God-Talk: Towards a Feminist Theology* (Boston, MA: Beacon Press, 1983).

Rupp, Gordon, *The Righteousness of God* (London: Hodder and Stroughton, 1953).

Saunders, E. P., *Paul and Palestinian Judaism* (Minneapolis: Fortress Press, 1977).

Schleiermacher, Friedrich, *The Christian Faith*, edited by H. R. MacKintosh and J. S. Stewart (Edinburg: T&T Clark, 1976).

Sobrino, Jon, *Christianity at the Crossroads: A Latin American View* (London: SCM Press, 1978).

Spence, Alan, *Christology: A Guide for the Perplexed* (London: T&T Clark, 2008).

— *The Promise of Peace: A United Theory of Atonement* (London: T&T Clark, 2006).

Thatcher, Oliver J. and Edgar Holmes McNeal, editors, *A Source Book for Medieval History* (New York: Scribners, 1905).

Tertullian, *On Modesty, ANF*, vol. 4.

Vermes, G., *The Dead Sea Scrolls in English* (London: Penguin Books, 1979).

Webster, John, editor, *The Cambridge Companion to Karl Barth* (Cambridge: Cambridge University Press, 2000).

— *Karl Barth*, second edition (London: Continuum, 2004).

Wright, Tom, *The Climax of the Covenant: Christ and the Law in Pauline Theology* (Minneapolis: Fortress Press, 1993).

— *Justification: God's Plan and Paul's Vision* (London: SPCK, 2009).

— *Paul: Fresh Perspectives* (London: SPCK, 2005).

— *What St Paul Really Said* (Oxford: Lion Publishing, 1997).

INDEX

1 Chronicles
  15.20–22 135
2 Chronicles
  5.10 23, 49, 84
  5.21 33
2 Thessalonians
  1.7–8 23
Daniel
  9.16 156
Isaiah
  2.17 20
  25.9 20
Joel
  1.15 20
  3.14 20
Micah
  6.8 149
Acts
  2.36, 37 23
  26.28 29, 144
Galatians
  3.1–3a 143
  3.16 134
Hebrews
  10.26, 27 51
John
  1.1 117
  20.23 53
Matthew
  3.1 2, 21
  6.33 156
  10.40, 42 19
  13.24–30 18

  13.41 18, 23
  13.49 19
  16.27 23
  18.21–35 22
  18.6 21
  21.33–45 20
  22.1–14 19
  23.1–36 22
  25.1–13 20
  25.14–28 19
  25.31 19, 23
  25.31–46 36
Philippians
  2.12b, 13 38
  3.8, 9 67
  3.9b 142
Revelation
  19.11–16 23
Romans
  1.2–4 136
  1.16a, 17 altered 157
  1.17 40, 63, 67, 68
  2.1 26
  3.10, 20a, 21a 155
  3.19 150
  3.22 155
  4.5 NIV 1
  4.6–8 157
  4.16a 123
  5.1, 2 56
  5.9, 10 158
  5.12–19 135
  5.16b 157

8.30 86
9.8b 142
9.30, 10.3, 31 67
9.30b, 10.3, 31 155

absolute freedom 71
absolution 53, 54, 125
active (or personal)
    righteousness 66, 68–9, 73, 75,
    79, 88, 152
affections 95–6, 98
Albert of Brandenburg 61
almsgiving 36, 37, 153
Anselm of Canterbury 45, 93
apostasy 51
Aquinas, Dominican Thomas
    44–58, 73, 80, 93, 139,
    152–3
    and Augustine's
        justification 55–6
    justification and
        glorification 48–50
    mortal sin 50–2
    nature of justification 46–8
    penance 52–55
        problem with 56–9
    scholasticism 45–6
    Summa contra Gentiles 45
    Summa Theologica 45, 46, 54, 80
Arians 115, 116
Aristotle 44, 93
Athanasius 116
atonement 2, 32, 104, 105, 138, 155
Augsburg Confession 63, 75, 77
Augustine of Hippo 30–43, 71, 80,
    81, 85, 123, 139, 152, 153
    Against Julian 43
    The City of God 37
    Confession 5–8, 33, 38
    on divine grace 37–40
    The Enchiridion 32, 33, 34, 36, 37
    human predicament 31–2
    interpretation of atonement 32

justification, and Thomas 55–6
justification of faith 36–7
*On Man's Perfection in
    Righteousness* 34
On Nature and Grace 35, 39, 41
On the Grace of Christ 39, 40
On the Spirit and the Letter 35,
    40, 67
On the Trinity 32, 36, 37
on righteousness of God 40–1
on righteousness of the
    justified 33–5
on righteousness of the law 41
salvation 65
Seventh Homily on 1 John 153
theory of the nature of evil 6
and work of Jesus Christ 32–3
Aulén, Gustaf 155

baptism 20–1
Barth, Karl 108, 109–26, 153
    Church Dogmatics 111, 118, 120
    critique of
        Schleiermacher 109–11
    election of the Son 114–18
    on justification 121–4
    *Protestant Theology in the
        Nineteenth Century* 110
    on reconciliation 118–21
    response to liberalism 111–14
    view on sin 118, 119
Beveridge, Henry 78
Bible 33, 91, 110, 112–13,
    115–17, 122, 149
black theology 148
blessedness 101–2, 104
Brunner, Emil 109
Bunyan, John 73
    Pilgrim's Progress 8

Callixtos 51
Calvin, John 75, 76–91, 120,
    152, 154

debate with Catholicism over
  justification 91
on faith 80–2
in good works 84–7
as a humanist scholar 77–8
*Institutes of the Christian
  Religion* 77, 78, 79, 80, 81, 82,
  83, 85, 86, 87, 91, 152
on judgment of reason 76–7
on justification 79–80
right attitude 82–4
union with Christ 78–9, 152, 153
Catholic perspective, on
  justification 87–90
Chalcedon 120
changing world-view,
  challenges of 92
Charles V 10
children, treatment of 21
church community 128
community of faith 103
The Community Rule 157
Cone, James H. 147–8
confession 7, 20–1, 53, 74
Copernicus, Nicolaus 93
coram deo 64, 69
corporate sin 22
covenantal nomism 129, 137
cross 69, 133, 137

Dante Alighieri 8–9
  The Divine Comedy 8–10
Day of Pentecost 23
Denifle, Henry 68
dikaiosune theou 155
divine and human natures, relation
  between 120–1, 142
divine forgiveness *see* forgiveness
divine grace *see* grace
divine speech-act 113
Doceticism 121
Donatist controversy 37, 51
Dunn, James 130

Eastern Church 2, 7, 59
election of the Son 114–18, 122
empiricism 94
Enlightenment 91, 104
epistemology 93
Erasmus, Desiderius 71, 77
  Diatribe on Free Will 71
estrangement from God 5
eternal life 37, 49, 50, 52, 55, 74,
  86, 90, 151, 153–4
euaggelion 135

fair judgement 10
faith 48, 55, 56, 70, 76, 86, 88,
  94, 123, 132, 134, 139, 142,
  152, 153
  in God 96–7
  justification of 36–7
  and love 43, 48, 81
  and reason 44
Farnese, Alessandro
  (Pope Paul III) 10
Feminism 148
final judgement 3, 4, 10, 17, 18, 21,
  22, 23, 36, 48, 49, 56, 75, 84,
  89, 95
forgiveness 42, 43, 46, 47, 54, 57,
  74, 80, 84, 86, 106–8, 121,
  122, 139, 152
free-will 5–6, 31–2, 47–8, 71, 87

Galileo 93
Gentiles 27, 140
Gibherti, Lorenzo 13
glorification, justification and
  48–50, 55, 57, 153
God's saving act 1, 48, 55, 70,
  79, 108, 113, 114, 123, 141,
  156, 157
God's Word *see* Word of God
God-consciousness 97, 99, 100,
  101, 102
good works, for salvation 84–7

Gospel 18, 19, 23, 34, 38, 40, 42, 60, 64–5, 67, 79–81, 83, 110, 112–14, 117–18, 123, 125, 132, 137
grace 36–40, 57, 65, 88
graciousness 17, 57, 142
Graeco-Roman, moral subculture 26

Hampson, Daphne 148
Hays, Richard 130
hell 8–10, 11, 13–15, 22
Hermas 51
Holy Spirit 36, 40, 41, 103, 113, 123–4
hope 88
Hugh of St-Cher 61
human accountability and guilt, awareness of 146–50
human faith *see* faith
human free-will *see* free-will
human plight 15, 16, 24, 71–2, 119, 146
human predicament 4, 5–16, 28, 31–2, 42, 127, 137, 146
humanism 62, 92
humility 83

imputation of the righteousness 72, 75
in abstracto 117
incarnandus 117
incarnation 121
indulgences 60, 61, 62
intellectual challenges 94
internal repentance 53
Irenaeus 75
Islamic perception of the West 25
Israel 133, 134
iustitia dei 63

Jesus Christ 19, 20, 21, 22, 50, 69, 101, 103, 111, 113, 114, 116–20, 125, 133, 136, 150

as the agent of Judgement 22–4
work of 32–3
Jews 26, 27, 129, 140
Johannes of Wesel 61
John the Baptist 20–1, 117
judgement, justification and 127–9
justificare 35
justified by faith 34, 72, 80, 157
see also faith
justified sinner 33

Kant, Immanuel 95
Kepler, Johan 93
Kierkegaard, Soren 112
kingdom of heaven 12, 18–20, 23

law, righteousness of 41, 68, 84
legalism 129
liberalism 111–14
love 35, 43, 48, 55, 88, 151, 153, 154
Augustine's view 36, 37
and faith *see under* faith
Luke 143
Luther, Martin 33, 59–75, 89, 139, 143, 152, 154
active righteousness 68–9
The Bondage of the Will 71–2
Commentary on Galatians 64, 66, 68, 69, 70, 72, 73, 74, 77
commentary on Jonah 65
on divine judgement 63–5
human plight 71–2
on Luther 70
Ninety-Five Theses 61–3
passive righteousness 69–71
on penance or repentance 62
on reason 77
righteousness of God 67–8
righteousness, kinds of 65–71
simul justus et peccator 72–3
Theses for Heidelberg Disputation 1517 64
Two Kinds of Righteousness 68, 70

Mark 20
Matthew 19, 20, 23
McCormack, Bruce 117
McGrath, Alister 35
mediatorial work of Christ 32, 33, 119
Melanchthon, Phillip 75
mercy 56, 58, 70, 81, 100
merit 43, 50, 56, 69, 85, 88
messianic nomism 138
metanoieo 52
Michelangelo Buonarroti
    Last Judgement 10–13
miracles, and faith 94, 101
mortal sin 50–2, 53, 55, 56–7

nature of justification 46–8
New Testament 2, 23, 57, 84, 143, 146 *see also* Word of God
    divine judgement in 17–29
Niebuhr, Richard 108, 124

obedience 36, 75, 88, 124, 129, 134, 137–8
O'Donovan, Oliver 4
Old Testament 20, 149
    see also Word of God

pagans/paganism 25, 26, 35, 37
Palestinian Judaism 129
passive (or alien or external) righteousness 66, 68–71, 73, 75, 79, 88, 90, 152
Paul 4, 40, 66, 67, 75, 84, 123, 128–30, 134–7, 142, 144, 151
    argued in a letter he wrote to the Christians in Rome 30
    on faith 132
    on justification 154–8
    letter to the Romans 24–8
    on righteousness 67
Pelagian controversy 37–40, 139, 142
Pelagianism 89, 123

penance 52–5, 60
    problem with 56–9
personal sin 7
Peter 23
Pietism 96
piety 95, 98, 101, 111
pilgrim 50, 65
Piperno, Fra Rainaldo da
    Supplement to the Third Part 54
pistos christou 135
poetic justice 9
Pope Eugene III 59
Pope Gregory VII 59
Pope Leo X 61
Pope Paul III 10
Pope Urban II 59
post-baptismal sins 51
predisposing grace 88
Protestant Reformation 10, 62, 75, 92
Protestants 88
punishment 4, 9–10, 20, 98, 99, 125
purgatory 60

reason, judgment of 76–7
reconciliation 47, 118–21
Reformed dogmatics 75, 109, 112, 120, 125
relative justice 49–50
religious affections 95–6, 98
remission of sin 46–8
Renaissance 10–11, 13, 61, 91, 92–3
repentance 7, 42, 48, 50–4, 56–8, 62, 64
resurrection 16, 30, 32, 121, 122, 123, 134, 135, 136, 153
revelation 120
revelation of truth, and justification 4
reward 20, 37, 49
righteousness 1, 33, 38, 46, 47, 73, 74, 79, 83, 154, 155

created vs imputed 34
from god 150–2
of God 24, 30, 40–1, 63, 67–8,
    75, 78, 88, 121, 128, 136,
    139, 140, 145, 148, 152,
    155, 156, 157
of the justified 33–5
kinds of 65–7
of the law 68
natural capacity for 40
Rodin, Auguste
    The Gates of Hell 13–16
Romans, judgement in 24–8
Ruether, Rosemary 148

salvation 2, 3, 6, 7, 30, 32, 36,
    38, 44, 56, 58, 62, 72, 81,
    85, 113, 145
of God 156, 157
interpretation of 2
types 136–9
Saunders, E. T. 129, 136
    Paul and Palestinian Judaism 129
Schleiermacher, Friedrich 92–108,
    112, 114, 124
    The Christian Faith 95, 96
communication of
    salvation 102–4
faith in God 96–7
human spirutuality 94–6
on justice of God 98–100
on justification 106–7
Barth critique of 109–11
magical view of salvation 104–6
on redemption 100–2
on sin 97–8
scholasticism 45–6, 77
Scholz, H. 111
Scotus, John Duns 45
Second Crusade 59
Second Temple Judaism 130, 136–7
secularism 9, 10, 13, 15
self-revelation of God 113–14

self-centredness, of salvation 132
self-consciousness 96–7
self-righteousness 129
simul justus et peccator 72–3, 76
Son of Man 18–19, 23
Spence, Alan
    Promise of Peace 138
spirit-inspired prayer 90
supernaturalism 103, 104

talents parable 19, 20
temporal punishment/penalties
    54–5, 60–1, 62
tenants parable 20
Tertullian, Quintus Septimius
    Florens 51
Tetzel, Johann 61
Third Crusade 59
Torah 27
tradition 152–4
traditores 51
Trent 88–90
Trinitarian 113, 115–17

ungodly, justification of 28, 30–1,
    35, 46, 47, 48, 50, 55, 80, 90,
    139, 153
unmerciful servant parable 22

Vatican II 147
virgins parable 20
volition 39

Webster, John 111
wedding banquet parable 19
Western Christendom 62
Western Church 3, 127, 158, 159
wickedness 1, 6–7, 9–10, 11, 19, 22,
    85, 108
William of Occam 45
Word of God 33, 91, 110, 112–13,
    115–17, 122, 149 *see also*
    New Testament; Old Testament

wrath of God 24, 64, 119, 125
Wright, Tom 128, 130, 144, 145
    critique of the tradition 131–3
    on history, covenant and
        apocalypse 130
    Justification 132, 133, 134
    and justification in Western
        thought 139–40
    Paul: Fresh Perspectives 136

salvation, justifying through
    Israel model 134–6
salvation narrative 133–4
salvation types 136–9
on Western Church's interpretation
    of justification 140–3
What St Paul Really Said 128,
    131, 132, 133, 134, 136, 137,
    139, 140, 141, 142